TO WIN THE WEST

Co-published with:

Bible Society
~~Bible Society's vision to equip the people of God with the~~
resources to make the Bible accessible and relevant to today's
world. Bible Society can be contacted at Stonehill Green, Westlea,
Swindon SN5 7DG.

The Church Pastoral Aid Society,
Athena Drive, Tachbrook Park, Warwick CV34 6NG. CPAS is a
mission agency which exists to strengthen churches to evangelise,
teach and pastor people of all ages. It seeks through people and
resources to stimulate evangelism, equip and train leaders, advise
about ministry and make grants for mission and training.

To Win the West

MARTIN ROBINSON

MONARCH
Crowborough

First British edition 1996

British Library Cataloguing in Publication Data
A catalogue record for this book is available
from the British Library

ISBN 1 85424 251 2

Designed and produced by
Bookprint Creative Services
PO Box 827, BN21 3YJ, England for
MONARCH PUBLICATIONS
Broadway House The Broadway
Crowborough East Sussex TN6 1HQ.
Printed in Finland.

CONTENTS

INTRODUCTION

The very phrase, 'to win the West', contains within it a profound difficulty. What I intend to convey in such a title is a sense of hope, a spirit of adventure, a vision of what might be. But the very same words can also be understood as suggesting a particular methodology or programme. If the church is to engage in a new 'winning of the West', it must not be deceived by the seductive thought that somewhere there exists a cure-all potion that will somehow end the long experience of numerical decline in many Western churches. It can be tempting to think that an outstanding leader, or a new movement, or some other panacea will reverse the indifference of many in the West to the Christian message. But the historical record suggests that the change needed to win the West will be more fundamental than that.

If it is true that the changes which are required to produce a new winning of the West are so far reaching that it is beyond the power of any one individual, movement or method to produce them then there remains the opposite danger of demoralisation. We might be tempted to think that there really is nothing effective that we can do.

I want to suggest in the pages that follow that there is indeed much that we can do as individual missionaries to win the West, and that our effectiveness can be enhanced by better understanding the larger themes of our times. In this sense I am writing for the person that I picture as the thoughtful activist. Who is this 'thoughtful activist'? Put very simply it is that person who is concerned enough about mission to think creatively about the task and who is also willing to be engaged in the task.

Three different but related kinds of concern need to attract the attention of the thoughtful activist. First, there are those issues which concern the culture itself. The recent history of Western culture has produced a huge antipathy towards the Christian message. Even when individuals have claimed to value Christianity for its moral teaching, the core beliefs of Christianity have often been rejected. Consider the testimony of one 'unbeliever' — the British author and playwright, John Mortimer:

> My unbelief doesn't mean that I could do without churches. As the slow queue shuffles up to the altar rails, Paul Nicholson says, 'You will be as much loved here whether or not you take Communion.' Whether that's true or not, I feel completely at home in this church at Christmas. Even as an unbeliever, I am part of a Christian civilization. Perhaps it's in its declining years, but Christianity has been responsible for me. The poetry I value, the art that is important to me, have existed in a Christian framework and can't be understood without a reference to Christian beliefs, even when they are rejected or used as a cover for more ancient pagan celebrations. The politics I have adopted come from the Sermon on the Mount by way of Victorian Christian Socialists and the preachers in Welsh chapels. For this reason, if for no other, Christianity has to be treasured and learnt; without it we couldn't understand Shakespeare or Milton. Without the Bible, in the form it took before the new translation wrecked it, spoken English is reduced to the meaningless waffle now heard in law courts and the Houses of Parliament. . . . So celebrating Christmas in the village church is at least as important as going in a procession to lay flowers on Shakespeare's grave.[1]

That rather condescending assessment of Christianity by Mortimer is one that most Christian leaders in the West will recognise and yet perhaps both he and we know that it is a view of Christianity that is now passing away. Christianity without a commitment to its core beliefs is simply unsustainable.

But what is it that causes such huge changes in our culture? Why is it that Western culture has been so hostile to religious belief of every kind in recent times? Why has religion recently re-emerged onto the agenda of the Western world? The serious missionary to the West needs to be able to understand such questions. A great deal of work has been undertaken in these areas and I have attempted to survey and analyse these questions in my recent work, *The Faith of the Unbeliever*.

The second set of issues concerns the ways in which the church in the West has developed in relation to the challenges that have come to it from the surrounding culture. The church has its own history apart from the tide of secular history. At particular times in the life of the church, secular history and church history have become so entwined as to be almost the same story. At other times the gap between culture and the influence of the church has been so profound that the history of the church seems to have almost no bearing at all on the secular flow of history, nor secular history on events in the church. But, whatever period of church history we consider, there are those internal movements which later prove to be decisive in the development of the church especially in relation to its missionary task.

As we consider the task of the church in winning the West we are forced to consider a period in history when the story of the church had been so identified with the story of Western expansion — empire, economic and technological domination of the world, colonialism and the subjugation of other cultures — that the success of Christian mission came to be identified with the success of the West in cultural, political, military and economic terms. It has therefore come as a profound shock to arrive at a situation where the ties of Christianity with the West are now significantly loosened.

As the twentieth century closes and the twenty first century approaches, the church is growing fastest in those countries which have been the target of Western expansion. The church in the West, and particularly in Europe, seems to have lost the confidence and faith which first fired the modern missionary movement. Western culture seems to have embarked on a long period of disowning its Christian spiritual heritage to such an extent that the West is now a focus for Christian mission.[2]

This separation between what had been the common destiny of the Western world and the Christian church requires us to look more closely at the recent story of the church. What are the major internal themes and developments within the church? How are movements within the church affecting the capacity or otherwise of the church to engage or re-engage in mission to the West? It is these fundamental questions that form the major focus of this book. In this sense *To Win the West* acts to some degree as a companion volume to *The Faith of the Unbeliever* already mentioned.

There remains a third set of issues which, although they are not the focus of this book, need to be remembered. If the task of the missionary is both to understand the culture to which they are sent and the developments within the church which impact the missionary orientation of the church, then the place where these two perspectives meet is of vital importance. For the most part, the local church is where these broader considerations have their actual effect. Strategy for mission needs to be formed in the context of a good understanding of the great themes of church and culture. The local church which has become a functioning missionary congregation stands at the point of this creative overlap. We could therefore represent the missionary church diagrammatically as follows:

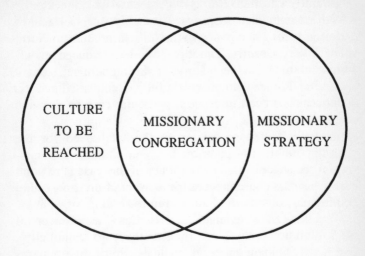

But the truth is, that many if not most local congregations are only now just beginning to struggle towards a missionary orientation. In that sense they are caught outside of any inter- action between the missionary concern of the church and an understanding of contemporary culture. For congregations such as these there is, as yet, no overlap. Much more work needs to be undertaken to help congregations make the leadership, organi- sational and conceptual leap from their present situation to that of a fully functioning missionary congregation. It may be that this third area will form the basis for a third book to complement the two that I have already mentioned.

Shortcomings

In penning these pages, I am all too aware of what has not been included. It is important to note that although there is an explicit intent to draw on particular historical themes, this is

not a book on church history or even mission history. Others
have written excellent works which deal with the church
histories of particular countries — notably Adrian Hastings
in relation to England[3] and Mark Noll[4] in relation to North
America. Very recently, Timothy Yates has produced an outstanding volume on the history of the modern missionary
movement.[5] Rather than provide a fully documented history,
my concern has been to argue a particular case by drawing
from church history.

Essentially that case relates to the vital need for the
broadest possible co-operation between Christians if mission is to be successful. The corollary of this case is to point
to the disastrous consequences for mission of division within
the Christian community. I am therefore arguing for what W.
R. Ward has called 'evangelical catholicity' as an essential
basis for mission to the West. In using the word 'catholicity',
Ward is describing a generous, inclusive spirit. In a remarkable essay on the development of the Baptist Union Ward
points to the connection between the emerging revival of the
late eighteenth century and a new view of evangelism:

> When in the 1790s, the barriers to evangelism at home and
> abroad began to collapse, the new panoramic view of history
> produced spectacular fruit in the movement know as Catholic
> Christianity, and induced in the evangelical Calvinists of Eng-
> land a mood of euphoria at the 'funeral of bigotry' . . . [6]

It is most definitely the 'funeral of bigotry' that is constantly
required if Christian mission is to be effective, particularly in
the Western world which has so often suffered from the
consequences of such narrowness. There often seems to be
a thin dividing line between personal empires and the kingdom of God. An obsession with personal empire usually
leads to small-scale numerical growth and a long-term
denial of mission. By contrast, a concern for the building
of the kingdom of God does not always lead to immediate
and obvious numerical growth, but it does lead to mission.

How and why mission takes place we cannot always know. Beyond our strategies, methods, ideas and creativity there lies the refreshing action of God who works by the Holy Spirit to surprise, confound and challenge us.

It is as well in every age to remind ourselves that although we are engaged in mission it is not, in the final analysis, our mission. Rather, we are called to share in God's mission and that is always more puzzling, uncertain and disturbing than any mission which we might invent. But, for the first time in many centuries, those of us who respond to the call to participate in the mission of God do not do so from the perspective of a monocultural, Western church but now as part of a global, multicultural, multiracial and multilingual family of nations. Mission is no longer Kipling's 'white man's burden' — was it ever really so? Rather, it is shared by millions of witnesses, known and unknown, who are inspired, directed and empowered by that same Holy Spirit.

In that sense, we are called not just to the one that we know, to Jesus Christ, but also to the unknown. There is a sense of mystery in mission which beckons us on to explore and discover riches as yet undreamed of. It is the mystery represented by the person of the Holy Spirit that in a sense guarantees the future of the church in the coming third millennium. It is my hope that something of the sense of wonder that an unfolding mystery reveals is also reflected in these pages spent exploring mission in the West.

Martin Robinson

Notes

1. John Mortimer, *Murderers and Other Friends* (Viking, 1994), pp. 256ff.
2. Note the concern of the Roman Catholic church for a new evangelisation of Europe. For a report on a gathering of

Catholic bishops to discuss this task see, 'A New Evangelization', *One World*, (March 1992), pp. 6ff.

3. Adrian Hastings, *A History of English Christianity 1920–1990*.
4. Mark Noll, *A History of Christianity in the United States and Canada*.
5. Timothy Yates, *A History of Christian Missions in the Twentieth Century*.
6. W. R. Ward, *Faith and Faction*, p. 207.

CHAPTER ONE

TRAVELLING WEST

Until very recently Christianity has been described by many of its detractors as an almost exclusively Western religion. This perception has often perplexed those Christian communities outside the West whose unbroken history of Christian devotion predates the activities of St Columba. It is worth reminding ourselves that there has been a thriving indigenous Christian community in India for far longer than there has been any Christian witness in the countries of Northern Europe. The indigenous African church in Ethiopia is far older than the organised church in England. Indeed the missionaries that first came to Great Britain owed their inspiration and vision to the spirituality of the church in North Africa. Why is it then that the conversion of the West has come to utterly dominate the history of the Christian church for more than a millennium?

Mission from the East

Few, if any, could have predicted that the message preached by an obscure preacher in a relatively insignificant corner of the Middle East would have travelled from the East to the great cities of Europe. At first sight, the mission of Jesus was hardly an outstanding success. His public ministry lasted only three years. During that time he assembled a relatively small group of followers. The inner core, the Twelve, were not representative of the society to which Jesus spoke. Many of them had known each other before they became disciples and some were members of the same family. The majority came from a particular region of Palestine. It seems that their understanding of the mission to which they were called was rather incomplete before the end of the public ministry of Jesus. Their teacher seemed to fail in his task. He attracted public opprobrium and his public ministry ended with a humiliating execution. To the first disciples contemplating the death of Jesus it all seemed to be over before it had ever really begun. The only alternative seemed to be to return to the trades they had known before, in the case of Peter and some of his other companions, to the business of fishing.

But the resurrection appearances of Jesus heralded an unexpected and new beginning. It was not the earthly Jesus but the resurrected Lord who issued them with the Great Commission as represented by Matthew 28 — the instruction to go and preach to all nations. The immediate consequence of the apostolic preaching following the death and resurrection of Jesus was the re-ignition of the mission of Jesus in the context of a dramatic and intercultural revival movement. Large numbers responded, but more significant than the sheer numerical growth was the extent to which cultural, linguistic and religious barriers began to be crossed. The church began to realise that the inclusion of those beyond the house of Israel was not merely a by-product of their main preaching activity but bore an intimate relationship to the message itself. The inclusion of all nations actually authenticated the message that was entrusted to them.

The explosion of growth that followed the events of Pentecost caused the message of Christianity to travel in many directions. There was a strong church established in the area covered by present-day Iran. The message also travelled further north and was accepted by the Armenian people.[1] Tradition suggests that St Thomas travelled as far as India to preach the gospel. We do not know how accurate this tradition really is but we do know that there was a thriving church in India by the fourth century which continues to this day. We know also of the spread of the Coptic Orthodox church to Ethiopia, producing a Christian community which also exists to the present day. The church also spread to regions immediately to the east of the Roman Empire. However, despite these important centres of the faith, the major story of the Christian faith during the first four hundred years of its life was essentially the drama of the conversion of the peoples of the Roman Empire. This development took the church in an ever westward direction, first to Rome, and then to the most western tip of Europe — Spain.

Facing the philosophers

The early church within the Empire was almost always a church located in a city. There were some exceptions, but the great expansion of the church around the Mediterranean basin was initially focused on the major cities, many of which were located on the great trade routes. The population of these cities was usually cosmopolitan in nature. To be a Christian was to participate in an international community. Certainly there were many Jews in the first Christian communities, but there were many more who had been part of the 'god-fearers', those individuals from a variety of nationalities who had been attracted by the message of Judaism but who for a variety of reasons had never crossed the threshold and actually become part of the house of Israel.

This early church contained an intercultural and interracial ingredient. It was also a church in competition, not with one other faith but with a multiplicity of faiths and philosophies. These faiths and philosophical schools were often deeply embedded in particular nationalities and classes. Each social group tended to have its own cult. The only cult that transcended all social and national boundaries was the cult of Caesar. The content of that cult was sufficiently slight that it was possible to attach veneration for Caesar to almost any other belief.

It is all too easy to look back on the growth of the church during the first few centuries of its life and conclude that the success of the church in this context was almost inevitable,[2] but this is far from the case. The rampant pluralism of the ancient world was matched by a public commitment to values and practices which were entirely inimical to the Christian faith. This was not fertile soil simply waiting for a new message to arrive which would then be eagerly embraced. Those religious groups that were in competition with the Christian message were themselves powerful and significant. The world-view and plausibility structures within which these Mediterranean populations operated were not at all friendly towards Christian thinking.

If it is true that the progress of the Christian faith in the Empire was not inevitable, how was it accomplished? Contemporary accounts drawn from the first three centuries clearly indicate that the various Christian communities in the ancient world developed a reputation for their devotion, for their charitable deeds and for their courage in the face of persecution. Many thousands of Christians whose names we do not and cannot know gradually extended the life of the church by their individual faithfulness and witness. Many were able to carry their faith to new lands because of their occupation as soldiers, civil servants and traders. The impact of many ordinary witnesses should not be underestimated. The great achievement of Christianity as it moved west from its original place in Jerusalem was its ability to explain an essentially Jewish eschatological movement in terms of Greek cultural and intellectual categories.

The Christian faith conquered the State that persecuted and despised it because it both won the intellectual high ground and it withstood the rigours of persecution. The genius of Christian thinkers in the Patristic period enabled the church to take captive the glories of Greece and Rome, to utilise the best in that civilisation in the cause of Christ. The eventual conversion of the Roman ruling class to the new faith, together with the accompanying status accorded to Christianity as the official unifying religion of the Roman Empire, served to identify Christianity with a whole civilisation to such an extent that it was difficult to separate the two.

This westward shift carried with it a number of problems that were stored up for the future. The very success of Christianity in fusing the civilisation of the Empire with the cause of Christ tended both to marginalise and to weaken those expressions of the faith which lay outside of the boundaries of the Empire itself. As long as the Empire stood, the gradual westward progress of the Christian faith throughout the Empire was always likely. But just as inevitable was a situation of crisis when the unthinkable happened. The complete and relatively rapid collapse of the Roman Empire in the West not only called into question the civilisation which Rome had previously fostered and guaranteed; it also seriously compromised the mission of the church in Western lands. State approval had been such an effective means of moving mission forward throughout Western Europe that the church hardly knew what to do in the face of civil collapse. This crisis was all the more acute because the agents of destruction were more often than not pagans of a kind that Christianity had scarcely encountered before.

Debating the Druids

The arrival of many pagan tribes from the North and the East, Saxons, Angles, Franks, Huns, Lombards and others, did not result in the immediate collapse of every existing Christian community throughout Western Europe. What it did produce was a crisis of confidence with regard to mission. Even though some of these tribes had encountered the Arian form of Christianity, many still worshipped pagan gods. How could Christians reach out to peoples who were uneducated, illiterate, practised human sacrifice and worshipped out of doors, often in wild settings? The gods they worshipped were drawn from the elemental forces of the universe. These tribes were powerful and this carried the suggestion that their gods were powerful too.

Many Christians lived in the towns; Christianity was still largely an urban faith responded to by city dwellers. These new peoples were unused to cities and were organised on a tribal basis. The existing Christian communities felt powerless to evangelise these heathens and for the most part they did not do so.

Yet these newcomers to the West were evangelised and the story of their conversion is a complicated matter. It is a complex story not least because it took more than 800 years to accomplish. Between the first wanderings of St Patrick in 432 and the final conversion of the king of the last nation in Europe to be won to Christ, Jagiello of Lithuania in 1386, lies a fascinating and diverse mosaic of trial and difficulty. The strands of this enterprise are also diverse. Some nations were won through the missionary endeavours of Eastern Christianity. Others were initially brought to Christ by Christians who held to the Arian heresy and only later adopted a catholic understanding of the faith. Some were entranced by the learning of the centres of Christian civilisation in Italy and parts of France. Still others were encouraged to become Christians as part of complicated diplomatic initiatives at court level. Marriages and alliances figured prominently in such approaches. The spirituality of the monastic movement impacted some. The new monastic orders operated as missionaries on many frontiers for the gospel within Europe. The wandering Celtic missionaries were to be found travelling along the valleys of every major river system in Europe. Traces of their work can be found in the British Isles, through France, Northern Spain, parts of Switzerland and Germany, and even into Eastern Europe as far as Russia itself. Still other parts of Europe, notably Scandinavia, encountered Christianity by means of the highly dubious tactic of armed conflict with its resultant forced conversion.

The members of such missions used a bewildering variety of approaches. The emissaries of the Tsar of Russia who travelled to Constantinople were simply overawed by the worship they encountered in the Orthodox liturgy. The simple, winsome holiness and accompanying miracle-working powers attributed to the Celtic saints was effective in winning others. The tradition of scholarship and the link with the older glories of Rome and Greece spoke to some. Whatever the particular approach, the collective consequence of this second attempt to win the West gradually produced the single cohesive civilisation which became known as Christendom.

Encountering Islam

This second Christian evangelisation of the Western world was accompanied by an equally difficult encounter with Islam. Islam also intended to win the West and it seemed to be in a very strong position to do so. Not long after the former Western Empire had been invaded by barbarian tribes forcing its complete collapse, Islam began a campaign of conquest which brought the former Christian territories of Egypt, North Africa, and the lands which we know today as Israel, Syria, Iraq, Iran and Turkey under its influence. Even though some Christian populations, for example in Egypt, saw the Arabs as liberators, the position of the Christian church in those lands was changed forever by the expansion of Islam.

Islamic expansion in the East continued towards the West. By 715 the greater part of Spain was occupied by the Muslim Moors. Muslim armies had entered France, were in occupation of Sicily and were even marching through Italy. Although the Muslim armies were defeated in France, notably at the battle of Tours in 732, their occupation of Spain continued for hundreds of years. The years from 900 to approximately 1500 saw further pressure from Muslim armies in Greek territories and in the Balkans. Constantinople fell in 1453 and Turkish armies eventually reached the gates of Vienna itself.

Before the advent of Christendom the Christian community in Western Europe felt itself to be under considerable threat. There was scarcely any contact with Christianity in the eastern half of the former Roman Empire. By the year 900 Scandinavia had not been converted to Christianity, neither had Russia, nor large parts of Central Europe. With Spain largely in Muslim hands and with France and Italy feeling under military threat, the Christian cause seemed weak indeed. Not only was the Christian community relatively weak in terms of overall numbers and in political and economic influence but it was overawed in cultural terms by the growing brilliance of an Islamic civilisation which had inherited a great deal of the ancient world's splendour. The Muslim community controlled the great trading routes that linked the Far East with Europe and elsewhere. Muslim scholarship was at that time far in advance of anything that Western Europe was able to produce. It was therefore small wonder that Islam felt able to contemplate the eventual conquest of Western Europe and that Christians in Europe felt acutely aware of the reality of such a threat.

The fact that Islam did not invade Western Europe and that these same territories became ever more self-consciously Christian was vitally important in redefining Christianity's self-identity as a religion. The loss of Christian communities in North Africa, the Middle East and Asia Minor, together with the loss of contact with those Christian communities that remained as minorities and with those that existed in lands to the east and the south of Muslim influence meant that Christianity thought of itself more and more as a specifically European religion. What had once been a Mediterranean religion with a strong intercultural dimension became more and more a homogenous religion identified exclusively with a culture that was to emerge as Christendom.

Despite the rather spurious and temporary victories during

the crusades, Western Europe felt itself to be rather isolated as a region. Before the discoveries of European voyagers in the Americas and elsewhere, Europe felt its position as a peninsula of Asia, the constant repository of migrating peoples from the huge hinterland of central Asia. The voyages of the Portuguese, Italian and Spanish explorers were explicitly motivated by a desire to overcome that perceived isolation. The Americas were discovered as a by-product of an attempt to make contact with the East Indies, an attempt to discover a way round the stranglehold on trading routes exercised by Muslim peoples. The consequences for Europe of such voyages, the gradual emergence of that continent as the dominant civilisation in a new period of colonisation and expansion was to have huge implications for the exercise of mission. A largely static Christian world, now understood almost exclusively as a European faith, was at last able to break out of its cultural captivity. But before this expansion could take place, another phase of mission was to take place within Europe.

The close of Christendom

The intention of the Reformers was to deepen the conversion of those who lived within the boundaries of Christendom. They were all too aware that some of the methods that had been employed in the winning of the barbarian West to the cause of Christ had led to the submergence of paganism but not its eradication. The campaigns of the Teutonic knights with their programme of military conquest and forced conversion were amongst the more notorious means that had been employed to win the West. The Reformers suspected, rightly in some cases, that the church had too easily baptised superstition as well as pagans. Anton Wessels comments:

> According to the historian Jan Romein, medieval Christianity was only a thin veneer. Only in the time of the Reformation in the sixteenth century was the northern part of Europe really Chris-

tianised. Others have also pointed out that before the Reformation and the Counter Reformation 'early modern popular culture in Europe had fundamentally remained "pagan animist".'[3]

It was no accident that many of the early Reformers were teachers, lawyers, monks and clerics. They were educated people whose knowledge of Latin gave them access to the pages of Scripture and the writings of the early church Fathers. Their desire to finally win the West at a deeper spiritual level, especially by making the Scriptures available to ordinary people, drove their concern for the reform of the church.

But the desire to reform Christendom contributed to the demolition of Christendom. While Reformers and Counter Reformers were engaged in propaganda and actual warfare with each other, new discoveries in the fields of science and philosophy were calling into question some very basic assumptions with which the medieval world had worked. These discoveries did not need to call into question the convictions of Christian faith, but the credibility of Christianity in relation to its use of political power had certainly been called into question as a consequence of the turbulent years of religious disputation and warfare.[4] The rise of new social and political classes, coupled with the arrival of new ideas about the operation of the universe, helped to force a reassessment of the role of religion in society.

The development of the modern nation state in Europe from the beginning of the seventeenth century onwards gradually ended the dominance of the church in political affairs. Most nations still had strong State churches which were interwoven with the fabric of the State, but those churches were there to serve the interests of the State and were not able to exercise the influence that they had enjoyed in medieval society. Moreover, in Protestant Europe, especially in England and its colonies, the State church had competitors in the form of the Nonconformist churches which offered a different vision of what it meant to be a Christian in society.

As the concept of Christendom was gradually dismantled, European society, now extended in to the Americas, was left without a clear vision of its future, although it drew its intellectual inspiration from the two sources that had been mediated to it by the channel of Christendom — the Bible and the classical world. The old paganism was either dead or overlaid by Christianity, but opposition to Christianity was far from over. In an intellectual climate which had wearied of religious intolerance, inspiration from the classical world of Greece and Rome took new forms. The period that we call the Age of Reason or the Enlightenment, sought to construct a world-view which was not dependent on the authority of the Bible or the church. The intellectual world-view that would usher in the modern world was being formed in this crucial period of time. Many of those who participated in this process were themselves devout Christians. This was not a movement which was intentionally anti-Christian but there were certainly those within it who did take such a stance. The claims of the Enlightenment had the potential to be used to wage war on the Christian church.

The hostility of some within an intellectual elite would not have mattered quite so much to the Christian community except that these attacks were mounted against a more general background of indifference to Christian faith. At a popular level it seemed as if the religious fervour of an earlier age had been replaced by an apathy, if not an antipathy, towards Christianity. The entire collapse of Christianity as a religion was predicted by some. The early and middle years of the eighteenth century represented a low point for the world-wide Christian community similar in seriousness only to that time before the full flowering of Christendom, when the twin threats of Islam and the barbarians threatened to extinguish the fire of Christianity altogether.

That this did not happen is testimony to the power of a series of religious revivals which began in the middle of the eighteenth century and continued in a variety of forms until the early years of the nineteenth century and in some Western countries up until the very end of that century. It was the energy that flowed from these revivals which largely fuelled the most astonishing expansion of Christianity that the church has ever witnessed. The Western captivity of Christianity was to lead in the nineteenth century to the Western export of the faith and eventually in the twentieth century to a situation where Christianity genuinely returned to its international, inter-racial and intercultural roots.

Dilemmas for mission

There can be little question that the Western church rejoices in the extent to which Christianity has been given away by the Western world to the rest of the world. It does not rejoice at all in the degree to which Western culture has abandoned the Christian faith and now seeks to live without it. Yet if the history of the church teaches us anything at all, it should teach us not to despair. The process by which the West has become yet again a mission field and the relationship of that fact to the wider story of mission is explored in more detail in succeeding chapters. My immediate concern in this chapter is to emphasise that the concern expressed in the title of this book — the winning of the West — is not an entirely new phenomenon. The West has had to be won for Christ before, not once but many times. Before we proceed to look at contemporary concerns we need to consider the lessons or dilemmas that already flow to us from the experiences of mission in the West to date.

Even before the advent of the modern missionary movement it was clear from the history of the church before the nineteenth century that certain dilemmas frequently emerged each time the church needed to rethink its mission. David Bosch helpfully points to six key paradigms with which the church has worked during the course of its missionary enterprise.[5] They are as follows:

1. The apocalyptic paradigm of primitive Christianity.
2. The Hellenistic paradigm of the Patristic period.
3. The medieval Roman Catholic period.
4. The Protestant (Reformation) paradigm.
5. The modern Enlightenment paradigm.
6. The emerging ecumenical paradigm.

The modern missionary movement as exported by the West has drawn heavily on the modern Enlightenment paradigm. The benefits of modernity — medicine and education — were transmitted as if they were part and parcel of the gospel message. Bosch calls the paradigm into which we are emerging 'the ecumenical paradigm'. It is too early to know whether he is correct in his assessment of the character of the coming paradigm. Frankly, I doubt it. I don't know what it might eventually be called, but my conviction is that the new paradigm will increasingly reflect the important fact of Christianity's growing intercultural character. To some degree, it might be called 'the Pentecostal paradigm', not in any denominational sense but because the Scripture tells us that the Spirit has been poured out on all flesh.[6] It is this single reality that allows and even compels the gospel to take on a variety of cultural clothes. Our close involvement with the recent paradigm of the Enlightenment and our uncertainty about the nature of the new paradigm means that we can identify the missionary dilemmas which have faced the church in the past from the first four paradigms listed by Bosch. What might these dilemmas be? Four come readily to our attention.

1. Entanglement with privilege

Christianity often begins life in a new culture as a religion of slaves, of the poor and of the underprivileged. It is an astonishing testimony to the power of the message of the redemption contained within Christianity that many of those who are poor become redeemed not just in a spiritual sense but in a social and economic sense also. It is often commented on that the children and grandchildren of the newly converted poor become doctors, lawyers and teachers. But the progress of Christianity in a given society is not entirely ~~characterised by the social progress of its adherents. The~~ gospel message also draws those from more privileged backgrounds. Malcolm Muggeridge, in his television portrait of the work of Mother Theresa in Calcutta, was particularly struck by the way in which young girls from high-caste Hindu backgrounds in South India came to work with the poorest of the poor, quite literally the untouchables, in the North of India after their conversion to Christianity. The attraction of the Christian message to wealthier and privileged segments of society extends also to the inclusion of those with fine minds. Great thinkers, writers, artists and musicians have offered their gifts to the cause of Christ at times when the spiritual tide of Christianity has risen high.

The involvement of a whole society in the Christian cause is both a goal of mission and a problem for mission. For example, the experiment of Christendom was an attempt to answer the question, 'What does it mean to attempt to apply the gospel to a whole society?'[7] The solutions contained great contradictions. On the one hand it brought a degree of popular piety which held society together in a very attractive and colourful fashion. The charm of Chaucer's *Canterbury Tales* conveys a society very much at ease with itself and its surroundings. On the other hand, the view of the Papacy adopted by Pope Julius II in the early sixteenth century astonished many. He saw himself as a Renaissance Prince and rode at the head of his armies wearing armour and a sword. It is difficult to reconcile the vision of Julius II, reliant on military might, with the humble obedience of Jesus of Nazareth. The entanglement with power and privilege, with success and honour, both helped and hindered the Christian cause. The problem of such compromise has been very real for the church in the West, not because Western

Christians are inherently more corrupt than Christians else-where, but because the progress of the gospel has allowed such opportunities to arise. It is a problem waiting to arise for Christians in other lands.

2. The challenge of renewal

The history of the Christian church demonstrates very clearly a pattern of spiritual intensity followed by a gradual decline to the point where the church stands in need of renewal. The very success of the church in penetrating every level of society with the Christian message almost guarantees both piety and apathy.

Two stories are told to explain the origin of the tradition of ringing a bell at a certain point during the mass. One story suggests that originally it was the main bell in the tower that was rung and that it was done in order to communicate to those who were too ill to come to church that the moment had arrived for them to eat the consecrated bread that had already been brought to them. In this way they could share in the worship of the church in a beautiful way. As you might imagine, that is the pious story.

The second story is that people often wandered in and out of the service, especially since it was in Latin and could not be understood by most. All kinds of business would be conducted outside the walls of the church as the service proceeded. The bell was rung to signal to those who were meeting with each other outside the building that this was the moment to return in order to receive communion. Which story is true? I suspect that both are. These stories remind us that piety and profanity have probably existed in equal proportions in the church during its long and sometimes meandering history.

Renewal has come in the past by means of a wide range of movements, from the fervour of those who have expected the imminent return of the Lord and who have engaged in ecstatic experiences of various kinds, to those who have sought to withdraw from the world in quiet, reflective medit-ation. But however it comes, renewal is often just as controversial as revolution. The involvement of the church with the normal everyday structures of society tends to insulate the spirituality of the Christian community from the kind of radical encounter which disturbs and challenges. Even though the description of various church commu- nities as reflecting secular power structures can be dismissed as sweeping generalisations, the caricatures sometimes con- tain the ring of truth. There have been times when the Church of England has resembled the Conservative Party at prayer. In the same way, the Nonconformists have been the Liberal, or even occasionally the Labour Party at prayer. Some elements of the religious right in America are today repre- sented as the Republican Party at prayer. Such entrenched interests do not always welcome spiritual renewal.

It is an observable fact that renewal often brings both controversy and division in the church. It is usually far from the mind of those involved in renewal that division will be the outcome. Indeed the expelling from the church of those involved in renewal tends to ensure that the church which is encouraging the exit will be less affected by renewal, at least for a time. Division hinders renewal and yet renewal tends to promote division. The problem of how to lead the church so that its mission can be strengthened by renewal without major division resulting is a continuing dilemma for Christian leaders.

3. The need for unity

The divisions of the church, first between its Orthodox Byzan- tine form and the churches of Persia, Syria and Egypt and then secondly between the Western Catholic and Eastern Orthodox churches, are sometimes cited as a major reason for the progress of Islam in those parts of the Mediterranean basin where Christianity was strongly established before the coming of Islam. These divisions were exacerbated by cultural and poli- tical factors as much if not more than by any doctrinal issues.

The increasing divisions of the Western church following

the Reformation are seen by some as a major cause for the hostility of an increasingly secular culture to the Christian faith. Quite simply, the divisions within Christendom were seen as undermining the credibility of a faith which spoke of forgiveness, healing, reconciliation and peace. Even apart from the apparent scandal caused by disunity, the practical consequences of a divided church have been felt by many Christians to be a major hindrance to the work of mission. The Ecumenical Movement saw from the beginning the relationship between unity and mission.

Nor has disunity been caused only by disagreements on doctrine between Christians who might otherwise have belonged to the same church. The growth of a cultural diversity within the Christian family has given rise to expressions of faith and worship which Christians from another culture find difficult. At least one African church has a prohibition against swimming in its statement of faith. Just when is something a matter of opinion about which Christians can legitimately differ and when is it of the essence of the faith?[8]

The growing diversity of the faith makes it extraordinarily difficult to conceive of a situation where the church is ever one entirely united body again. Does this really matter? Or is it the case that what matters more is a spiritual unity? In a time when the most serious divisions in Christianity are no longer denominational but cut across all denominations, isn't it also the case that there are informal patterns of unity which also disregard denominational affiliation? Does the question of what we mean by Christian unity need to be radically rethought?

There seems to be a basic dilemma for a church in mission. Some form of unity seems to be both a pragmatic and ideological aid to mission while at the same time, the more that evangelism and mission takes place across cultures and to new, unreached groups, the more bewildering becomes the range of churches that form some part of the Christian family. Our ecumenical age is producing more denominations than ever and this flowering of the unfamiliar seems to be an expression of life much more than a sign of decline and disagreement. Nor is the cutting edge of this growth to be found with the clergy. It is often lay-led movements that produce the most culturally diverse and appropriate expressions of the faith.

4. The role of believers

Within Christendom, where each person in society had a clearly defined role, the distinction between clergy and lay people was taken for granted. The job of clergy was to run the affairs of the church and to support the laity in their involvement in the world. The duty of lay people was to attend worship, support the church financially, pray and live a moral life in the sphere of their employment, family and community. As Bosch has so ably demonstrated, the church now lives two or three paradigms removed from such a medieval catholic paradigm and yet views of the relationship between clergy and laity have sometimes remained frozen in an earlier paradigm.

One of the watchwords of the Reformation was that of the 'priesthood of all believers'. According to the Reformers, every believer had a ministry which needed to be exercised within and without the church. In practise, this particular tenet of Reformation fervour never gained any serious ground within the life of the church. The jealous guardianship of the sacraments continued in many, though not all, Protestant churches. Even in the less sacramental branches of Protestantism the role of clergy was often enhanced by the importance placed on preaching and the implied claim that only trained experts could really interpret the Bible. While it was true that the Reformation opened the Bible to all, it was often opened only as a devotional aid; its actual exposition remained as much in the hands of Protestant clergy as the Latin Bible had been the preserve of the priest.

Successful mission has often been a lay enterprise and, as recent studies are beginning to reveal, the place of women has been of particular importance. The growth of mission both demands and encourages a vigorous response from lay people to the point where mission often produces a reassessment of the relationship between clergy and laity. It is the claim of some Catholic writers that the Catholic church would hardly exist in some parts of the world apart from the very active involvement of lay people. It would seem that, although it is not much discussed in the hierarchy of the church, the administration of the sacraments and other duties normally conducted only by the priesthood, are regularly conducted by lay people.

If there is any theme at all that is distinctively that of the twentieth-century church, it is that of the emergence of the laity, not just as a more active adjunct to the professional priesthood, but as priests themselves. The new missionary agenda is forcing a reconsideration of the relationship between laity and clergy. The implications of that new relationship for other themes within the life of the church are considerable. Baptism and Eucharist, the meaning of ministry and its relationship to gifts, the question of training and education, and the issue of the way in which the church relates to the world, these and many more matters will need to be reconsidered in the light of a new missionary paradigm which places the laity much more clearly at the centre of the life of the church.

These four themes at least will emerge in various forms during the next ten chapters. The church, having travelled almost exclusively West for more than a millennium, has now journeyed elsewhere. That wider intercultural journey is challenging the categories of theological, ecclesidocical and missiological thought which have been defined so far almost entirely by Western thought structures. The results of that rethinking can help the Western church to reconsider the field on its doorstep. The West has had to be converted a number of times before. We can learn from that history as well as from the contemporary lessons of Christianity in other parts of our world.

Notes

1. It is claimed that the conversion of the Armenian nation marks the first occasion when a whole people, including rulers, became Christian.

2. A good number of histories of early Christianity do tend to treat the first few centuries as if it was inevitable that Christianity would become the dominant faith. But this is to interpret history through the eyes of what has happened rather than to take seriously what might have taken place. A constant theme is that Christianity arrived at a time when conditions were ripe for its acceptance. One example of this approach is to be found in J. G. Davies, *The Making of the Church*, (Mowbray, 1983).

3. Anton Wessels, *Europe: Was it Ever Really Christian?*, p. 4.

4. This thesis is argued strongly by W. Pannenberg in *Christianity in a Secularised World*.

5. David Bosch, *Transforming Mission: Paradigm Shifts in Theology of Mission*, pp. 181ff.

6. Acts 2:17.

7. Jacques Ellul debates the value of Christendom as a living society in *The New Demons*.

8. See the debate in Hans Küng, *Christianity, the Religious Situation of Our Time*, pp. *xxi* ff. and pp. 1–58.

CHAPTER TWO

THE IMPACT OF EDINBURGH

At the beginning of our present century, it was possible for European and American Christians of every persuasion to look back on the previous century with some satisfaction. It had been a century of tumultuous change in almost every sphere of human activity. The arrival with some force of the industrial revolution had brought whole new industries into being. New discoveries were being made in science and technology. Political change had brought emancipation to whole sections of the population which had previously been excluded from the political process. The benefits of at least elementary education had touched virtually everyone in the population. Expanding and confident cities echoed the growth in influence and power of Western culture and economies. As the world outside of Europe and North America was encountered it was also largely tamed. Even when a foreign land did not become part of a European empire, French, German, Dutch, Spanish, Portuguese or British, its economy was often utilised in order to benefit the new Western world order. In the midst of these vast changes, the church had managed to develop and strengthen its influence in the varied societies of the West.

The beginning of the nineteenth century had not looked nearly as promising for the church as did the prospects at the end of that century. In England, as in most other Western lands, the eighteenth century had been so disastrous for the church that its future was certainly in doubt. As the historian Adrian Hastings puts it:

> The Church of Jane Austen was a profoundly secularised one. That is where the nineteenth century began. 'The Church as it now stands no human power can save', was Thomas Arnold's judgement. In fact the next fifty years witnessed an amazing recovery of religion both Established and dissenting.[1]

Revival fire

The recovery to which Hastings refers was all the more remarkable because the process of industrialisation removed millions of people from their familiar surroundings and cast them adrift in what was often the social abyss of the new cities. The church, used as it was to a more rural setting and pastoral rhythm, was completely unprepared to respond to this dramatic new challenge. The underlying theme which made it possible for the church to prosper in this new setting was the astonishing power and vitality that flowed from the evangelical revivals of the late eighteenth and early nineteenth centuries. The first flow of revival began almost simultaneously in the United States and Great Britain. The connecting chord was the ministry of George Whitefield, who greatly influenced the development of the revival on both sides of the Atlantic. The American revival of this period (the 1740s) is often referred to as the Great Awakening while the British manifestation is usually thought of as the Wesleyan revival.[2]

While it is certainly true that this revival movement sometimes broke out in city and industrial settings, for example amongst the miners of Kingswood near Bristol, the size of city populations and of industrial communities was nothing like what they would become during the nineteenth century. A great deal of the impact of this first revival was felt in the small towns and villages of rural America and England. But the communities that were forged in the heat of revival proved to be powerful enough to make the transition to the larger town and city settings which became the normal home for many citizens in the nineteenth century.

The initial impetus of the mid-eighteenth century revival might have died away without leaving any lasting mark on a dead and dying eighteenth-century church beyond the creation of a few new and still relatively small denominations. But successive waves followed and carried the tide of revival well into the first half of the nineteenth century. In America, a significant eruption of revival in the early nineteenth century, known as the Second Great Awakening, left an indelible mark on the developing Midwest just as the First Great Awakening had impacted the Eastern Seaboard of the United States. There was no direct equivalent in Britain to this movement but smaller and local revivals did help to strengthen and develop that which had begun much earlier.

The converting zeal of these revivals not only added to the numerical strength of Christianity throughout the nineteenth century but, more importantly, they changed the character of both church and society throughout this period. In England, evangelicals made their mark both on the Church of England and on Nonconformity. As Derek Tidball remarks, before the revivals, the Nonconformist or Dissenting churches had become both ' . . . small and stagnant and not a few had taken the road to Unitarianism'.[3] They were, after all, the losing party following the Restoration of the monarchy in 1660 and had lived in the shadow of that defeat for more than a hundred years. The existing denominations such as the Baptists and the Congregationalists slowly began to benefit from the life that the revivals brought. But much more decisive was the powerful addition of the many vigorous Methodist connections which were the direct creation of the revival itself.

The established church, though losing a great deal because of the failure to keep Methodism within the Church of England, nevertheless began to be transformed by the activity of evangelicals in its ranks. Derek Tidball rightly points to the influence of Charles Simeon in helping to keep evangelicals loyal to the established church. Apart from the influence of his own ministry in Cambridge which impacted several generations of theological students, Simeon

> ... had the foresight to see the importance of securing a succession of evangelical appointments to parishes and so set up a Trust to purchase available patronages to ensure that this would happen. ... His influence touched many areas. Lord Macaulay spoke of it, probably rightly, as being far greater than any primate.[4]

Evangelicals of the early nineteenth century had a strong social agenda and sought to change society not just by advocating a strict personal moral code, but also by means of an active political involvement. The influence of the 'Clapham Sect' in introducing social reforms in such matters as the abolition of slavery, the reform of prisons, child welfare, education and labour reforms is well known. While many of these reforms were spearheaded by leading Anglican evangelicals, Nonconformists were active at a grassroots level in assisting movements for social reform such as the Trade Union movement, the Chartist movement, the Co-operative movement and the emerging Labour Party. These English developments were mirrored in the United States and in other European countries as Christianity sought to adapt itself to the new emerging reality of industrialisation and the political strength of an increasingly dominant Western culture.

The vigour of evangelical Christianity, while often setting the agenda for the wider church, also encouraged other expressions of the Christian faith to renew their life and witness. Both the Broad Church and the Anglo-Catholic wings of the Church of England were revitalised during the second half of the nineteenth century. Derek Tidball points to the effect of the philosophical influence of Romanticism on some evangelicals as producing a tendency towards a higher view of sacraments and liturgy.[5] At the same time, Roman Catholicism, having been changed by the impact of the Counter-Reformation, was beginning to recover its nerve, even in those parts of Europe and America where the legacy of the Reformation had left the Catholic church numerically weak. The nineteenth century saw the revitalisation of Catholic Mission Societies, many of which were created in England and the United States.[6] In part this recovery of confidence owed much to patterns of emigration. In England the small indigenous Roman Catholic community became vastly outnumbered after the 1840s by the arrival of Irish immigrants, attracted by the demand for new sources of cheap labour fostered by the industrial expansion of Great Britain.

By the end of the nineteenth century and the beginning of the twentieth century, the churches were able to look with a degree of self-congratulation on their respective achievements. In England, the nonconformists were at the height of their power. From humble working-class and lower middle-class origins at the beginning of the nineteenth century, the forces of Nonconformity had become one of the most powerful social, political and economic realities of the age. In particular, the political bond with the radical Liberal government of the Edwardian period demonstrated to the pleasure of Nonconformity that it was at last accepted in the mainstream of British social and political life. At the same time the Anglican church could feel that it had been able to respond successfully to the challenge of Nonconformity and that its radical church-planting initiatives of the second half of the nineteenth century had ensured its survival as a national church. During the same century, Catholicism in Britain had won itself the right to a legal existence and, although it might have been open to the accusation that it often constituted something of a cultural ghetto, it could nevertheless claim to have experienced not only survival but significant growth.

This remarkable adaptation to a new and powerful industrial society was also in large measure a response not only to changed social conditions but also to the intellectual environment produced by the Enlightenment of the earlier eighteenth century. The new colonial powers of the West were above all societies shaped by the fruit of the Enlightenment. The intellectual insights of rationalism together with the technological triumph of empiricism provided the power base for the newly dominant West. European and North American man was above all Enlightenment man, bound together by a common set of cultural assumptions that flowed from what had been a transatlantic development. The Christian churches of Europe and North America were also significantly influenced by Enlightenment perspectives.

The modern missionary movement

This self-understanding dramatically influenced that other great achievement of nineteenth-century Christianity, the emergence of the modern missionary movement. The historian Adrian Hastings helpfully traces the difference between the early missionary impetus of the church and that which has taken place in the modern era. He points out that the first few centuries of the Christian church were marked by a spontaneous expansion of the church that was not dependent on any one form or expression of the Christian faith. In particular, he notes that the early spread of Christianity took many cultural forms ranging across those found in India, Persia, Armenia, Egypt, the Hellenised Mediterranean and the Western reaches of Europe. This variety of cultural expression gave rise to what Hastings calls a 'horizontal catholicity'.[7] He contrasts this situation with the later 'vertical catholicity' which was developed by the Roman Catholic church in the post-Reformation period. This Western uniformity was fatally tied to the colonial expansion of Spain and Portugal.

The Protestant church was no less guilty of connecting mission with colonial power. The energy of the early revivals in the late eighteenth century produced a strong incentive amongst Protestants to engage in missionary activity beyond the boundaries of Europe and North America. Indeed some have traced the origins of the revival itself to the missionary zeal of the Mennonites who were to prove so decisive an influence on John Wesley. The concern for mission expressed itself as a determination to win souls for Christ regardless of geographical boundaries and to some extent with much less regard for denominational structures than had hitherto been the case. This feature of evangelical churchmanship expressed itself in the creation of a vast range of voluntary societies which frequently crossed denominational and geographical boundaries. In Britain such organisations as the London Missionary Society and the British and Foreign Bible Society were excellent examples of cross-denominational co-operation which had an evangelistic or missionary concern at their centre.

The same mix of denominational co-operation and world-wide concern for mission was exhibited in the creation of a large number of voluntary societies in the United States. The American Board of Commissioners for Foreign Missions (1810), the American Tract Society (1825) and the American Bible Society (1816) were just three examples of such societies.[8] The American Bible Society was particularly interesting in that it saw its task as reaching the 'destitute' settlements of the West as well as providing Bibles for the various foreign language groups arriving from Europe. In this sense, foreign mission and home mission were indistinguishable.

As foreign missions developed, the connection with a colonial mind set was all too evident. Roland Allen, writing as long ago as 1927, describes in some detail the failure of the dependency culture produced by Western missions. He pointed out that it was not just a question of money (seductive as that can be), but it was also a confusion as to the aims that were being proposed. It was all too difficult for many missionaries to make the distinction between making someone a Christian and attempting to encourage them to dress, talk, worship and think like Westerners.[9] Andrew Walls made the same point more recently when he contended that many who defended Christian missions in the nineteenth century did so on the basis that they were preparing Africans and others for 'civilisation' over and against the view that missions were a misconceived undertaking since Africans did not possess the mental capacity to benefit from the effects of European culture. Even when missions attempted to train indigenous leaders, the goal of much nineteenth century mission seemed to be to produce African clergy who would be identical to Western clergy in everything except colour.[10]

Yet despite these and many other obvious shortcomings, the missionary movement of the nineteenth century achieved astonishing successes. It is estimated that prior to William Carey's call to evangelise the world through mission, the percentage of the world's population claiming to be Christian stood close to 20 per cent.[11] This was a figure that was astonishingly close to that which prevailed at the time of Constantine. As we have noted already, the years between had seen battles with Islam and a change to the boundaries of Christian influence. Christian North Africa and much of the Christian Eastern Mediterranean had been lost to the church. New territories in the West and North of Europe and in the Americas had been won but the overall effect in terms of the world's allegiance to Christ and his cause had remained unchanged. But in a single century (1800–1900), the proportion of Christians in the world's population had grown dramatically to number a community one third of the population of our planet. Naturally, as Western Christians looked back on the nineteenth century's achievements in mission, they did so with some pride in past accomplishments and with eager anticipation to what might be achieved in the new century to come.

An ecumenical spirit

Despite the fact that the case for foreign missions had to be argued persuasively in the early days of the modern missionary era, by the end of the nineteenth century the case had largely been accepted. Almost every denomination had its own missions programme in addition to the activities of the interdenominational agencies. There is a case that those who were willing to argue against missions were also rather sectarian in their general outlook. This is not the place to make that case. However, it is much more readily accepted that many of those who owned a passion for mission combined that passion with a genuine desire to see Christians of various persuasions working in active co-operation to promote the cause of mission. The roots of what we might call an ecumenical spirit were themselves to be found in the origins of the evangelical movement itself. One historian of the ecumenical movement says of the revival:

> . . . its spirit and its underlying motives were always the same. Its passion was evangelism — evangelism at home and to the ends of the earth. One result of this passion was in evidence everywhere — the coming into being of societies, voluntary movements, or organisations, in which Christians of different Churches and different nations banded themselves together to win the world for Christ. As redeemed, they had a mission to proclaim redemption.[12]

Ironically, while it is true that the evangelical revivals of the nineteenth century had the effect of producing many new denominations, this result was much more frequently the outcome of practical problems, over-enthusiasm, impatience with or opposition from the existing churches. Strangely these new divisions did not accurately reflect the general character of the revival itself.

We can see the much more ecumenical flavour of evangelicalism in three distinct developments. The first is the creation of the diverse interdenominational societies already mentioned. The point about these societies is not just that they allowed Christians from many denominations to work together to achieve a particular pragmatic goal. Many societies were established in such a way that denominational sensitivities were recognised and overcome. One example of this process is found in the formation of the British and Foreign Bible Society. The charter lays down that a certain proportion of the Board must be Anglican and a certain proportion must not be Anglican — in the original context, they must be Nonconformists. The arrangement ensured that no one group could dominate. In the same way, the operation of the Board remained both pragmatic and inclusive in its spirit. So, for example, since the Society wished to have Quakers on its committees, and since Quakers found pre-arranged prayer offensive, the Society did not include prayer in its committee meetings until 1859, more than half a century after its formation!

The second is the lead that evangelicals took in the establishing of national schemes of unity between divided groups within particular confessions, for example amongst Baptists and Methodists, and also in the development of world confessional bodies. The nineteenth century saw the formation of six such major world confessional organisations or fellowships, Anglican, Presbyterian, Methodist, Old Catholic, Congregational and Baptist (although the first actual Baptist conference took place in 1905).[13]

The third is the formation of the Evangelical Alliance. Towards the middle of the nineteenth century, evangelical Christians in Switzerland, France, Germany, the United States, Scotland and England were all beginning to make moves towards what eventually became the Evangelical Alliance. In 1846 a meeting of 800 Christian leaders from fifty two different branches of the church in eleven countries met together to form an Evangelical Alliance which had individual and not denominational membership. The documents from those early years recognised its ecumenical potential and freely used the word 'ecumenical' to describe their activities.[14]

Co-operation in mission

The practical outworkings of the Evangelical Alliance help to demonstrate the intrinsic connection between a concern for mission and an awareness that such a concern inevitably meant the co-operation of Christians. One of the very first fruits of the Alliance was the promotion of united prayer during the week following the first Sunday in the year. These meetings were sometimes the only occasions when those from the major national churches, the historic Free churches and smaller denominations such as the Brethren would meet together for prayer. Inevitably the focus for such prayer was often that of a united witness to reach the world. It is therefore not surprising that the plan for the first International Missionary Conference held in 1854 was first suggested at an Annual Meeting of the British Alliance.

Although the Alliance itself never became the primary vehicle by which the desire to see co-operation in mission was carried forward, evangelicals continued the quest for united action in mission using a variety of agencies, most notably the Student Christian Movement (SCM). In the nineteenth century the SCM was a formidable evangelical force reaching intellectuals in the universities for the cause of Christ. Other organisations such as the YMCA and YWCA and the Student Volunteer Movement (volunteering for Christian mission) were also influential. It was often leaders from these movements that were to be found advocating co-operation between the denominations. The Student Volunteer Movement for Foreign Missions adopted as its slogan, 'The evangelization of the world in this generation'. Such a call inevitably stirred hearts well beyond the boundaries of that one movement.

The impetus to co-operate across denominational boundaries operated at two levels. At the institutional level, denominations and mission agencies entered into what were known as 'comity' agreements whereby new mission fields were assigned to particular missionary bodies in order to prevent competition and duplication of effort. At the local level, especially where 'comity' arrangements had not prevailed, missionaries on the field were often at the forefront of the desire for practical co-operation. Latourette points out that those who were sent as missionaries may not have had strong inclinations towards such co-operation before being sent but the experience of the mission field often overcame earlier reserve:

> Once transported from the setting in which the inherited confessional loyalties seemed an accepted and immutable part of the religious landscape, more and more missionaries came to believe that divisions among Christians were a scandal, a denial of the Faith.[15]

Those who were insistent on the importance of denomination and churchmanship while in Europe often found that they were able to make common cause with Christians of very different persuasion when on the mission field and faced with the challenge of non-Christian faiths.[16]

As national churches developed on the mission fields national Christians increasingly joined the chorus of discontent with what they often felt to be imported and irrelevant divisions in Christianity. Although by no means all missionaries or newly converted nationals felt strongly about the scandal of division, nevertheless those that did added their voice to the growing desire to co-operate in order that the task of completing the task of evangelising the whole world might proceed more effectively.

The widespread feeling towards practical missionary co-operation began to have growing practical expression in the holding of a number of important international missionary conferences. The inspiration for these events was almost as old as the modern missionary movement itself. In the very early years of the nineteenth century, William Carey himself had proposed the holding of an international missionary conference to be held at Cape Town in South Africa in 1810. This concrete suggestion never took place but as the nineteenth century progressed a number of other conferences were held. I have already referred to the first conference in 1854. Other such conferences took place in Liverpool in 1860, in London in 1878 and again in 1888. Another important conference was held in New York in 1900 with the title, 'The Ecumenical Missionary Conference'. These various events attracted increasingly large attendances and did so on the basis that most of the people present were individuals who had an interest in missions. Certainly, representatives of various missionary societies were present, but they did not predominate. In the early years of the twentieth century there came a growing conviction that it would be necessary to hold an international missionary conference that did have a representative basis.

The New York conference of 1900 had ended with a call to hold another conference in 1910, this time in Edinburgh. A committee representing British missionary societies was appointed to plan the 1910 event. It was this group that began to realise that a rather different kind of gathering was required if the aims of the conference were to be met. The personalities that drove the planning group were men whose lives had been shaped by a deep personal faith that emanated from the evangelical revivals of the nineteenth century. Two figures stand out above all others. Joseph H. Oldham, a former Scottish missionary to India, and John R. Mott, an American Methodist layman. These younger men, representative of a new generation of leaders, had developed their interdenominational leadership skills in the Student

Christian Movement. Oldham and Mott, together with others on the planning committee, realised that previous missionary conferences had fallen short of their objectives in creating a more united missionary endeavour for two principle reasons. First, as already noted, the earlier gatherings had been composed both of individuals with an interest in missions and of representatives from the missionary societies. This combination of delegates produced an atmosphere which suggested that the main purpose of these events was to allow the missionary societies to present and promote the cause of mission much more than to discuss practical means of co-operation. Second, the earlier missionary conferences had drawn almost entirely upon an evangelical constituency. The failure to reach beyond evangelical circles meant that almost by definition the degree of co-operation that could be elicited would be partly deficient.

But how could those outside of evangelical circles be persuaded to participate in what had seemed up until now to be an exclusively evangelical concern for completing the Great Commission? They quickly realised that the key to such a process lay in issuing invitations to Anglicans and especially to those in the Anglo-Catholic wing of the church. The Society for Promoting the Gospel (the SPG — later the United Society for Promoting the Gospel, the USPG) was especially important. Oldham and Mott were able to use their personal friendships developed amongst Anglicans through the Student Christian Movement to initiate this process. It was far from easy. Initially the SPG refused to be represented but much patient work not only helped to reverse this decision (they sent thirty four official representatives to Edinburgh), but others from many countries who were not evangelicals eventually accepted invitations to attend. The stage was set at last for a conference which was very close to the idea of one at Cape Town which Carey had had a century earlier.

The watershed of Edinburgh

Although it is certainly true that Edinburgh 1910 was a completely Protestant event it was not an exclusively evangelical conference. This single fact gave the event a character which was entirely different from all previous missionary conferences. The presence of a catholic view of the church, of its mission, its ministry and its sacraments, albeit found largely within an Anglican context, helped to produce an atmosphere in which it was possible to express the hope that in future days, members of the Roman Catholic and Orthodox churches would be able to participate in international missionary conferences such as Edinburgh. The climate of co-operation produced by such a breadth of representation clearly acted as an inspiration to many of those who were present at Edinburgh. Many delegates were subsequently to play leading roles in the development of missions thinking in their respective denominations.

But Edinburgh was different from other earlier events not just in its representation, but more particularly in its purpose. Certainly, the means by which delegates were invited reflected that different intent. Missionary societies were invited to send delegates in direct proportion to the amount of money that they expended on mission work amongst non-Christian peoples. Those societies engaged in proselytising within predominantly Christian nations were not invited. Although it is true that to invite delegates from missionary societies is not the same thing as to invite delegates from denominations, at least in Britain and America if not in continental countries, the relationship between denominations and missionary societies was very close. To invite a representative from certain missionary societies was to involve the denomination to which they were closely attached.

Edinburgh was intended as an event where work would be done. Its purpose was to enable the various societies to learn together, to think and inspire one another with concrete suggestions as to how mission could be better undertaken, problems overcome, resources marshalled, co-operation increased, and the new and younger churches strengthened. To this end, unlike all previous events, a huge amount of preparatory work was undertaken.

Some two years before the conference, eight Commissions were appointed to look at eight major topics and to prepare extensive papers to be considered by delegates before they arrived. Latourette tells us that the members of these Commissions were '. . . drawn from scores of countries and denominations'.[17] In order to solicit as wide a range of opinion on these topics as possible, John Mott wrote personally to more than 600 people all over the world asking them to consider a range of questions which he put before them. Their responses helped to induce an atmosphere of expectation and co-operation even before the conference began.

The eight Commissions looked at the following topics:

1. Carrying the gospel to all the non-Christian world.
2. The Church in the mission field.
3. Education in relation to the Christianisation of national life.
4. The missionary message in relation to non-Christian religions.
5. The preparation of missionaries.
6. The home base of missions.
7. Missions and governments.
8. Co-operation and the promotion of unity.

Those who contributed to the Commissions came from a large number of countries. But, because of the principle which lay behind the calling of delegates, namely the sending strength of mission societies, the overwhelming majority of those who attended came from the Northern hemisphere. In 1900 83 per cent of the world's professing Christians lived in Europe and North America. As Andrew Walls puts it, 'It seemed natural for the Conference to divide the world into missionized lands and lands not yet fully missionized'.[18] There was a total of 1196 delegates. Of these, 500 came from the United States and a further 500 from the United Kingdom. One hundred and seventy delegates were drawn from other parts of Europe, notably from the Germanic-speaking countries and Scandinavia. Just twenty six delegates came from every other part of the globe. Of these, some were missionaries from other Anglo-Saxon countries such as Australia and New Zealand. Only seventeen came from the younger churches in the lands that were to be evangelized. Fourteen of that number were chosen by the missionary societies in the West with which they were connected and three were specially invited by the Executive Committees in America and Britain. Not a single delegate was an African Christian!

For those who attended the Edinburgh 1910 Conference, the event was momentous. But the importance of Edinburgh was perhaps not so immediately clear to those who had not been directly impacted by the enthusiasm of the event. Latourette, together with other church historians, is certainly correct to point out that its significance has been more clearly seen as time has passed. Many have spoken of the event as a watershed. In what sense is that really true? Four developments that flowed from Edinburgh are sufficiently important to justify such a description.

First, Edinburgh gave rise to a great deal of practical co-operation in mission.

The final act of the conference was to create a Continuation Committee. The partnership of Mott and Oldham continued with John Mott acting as Chairman and Joseph Oldham as Secretary. The immediate actions of the committee were to hold a series of eighteen regional and three national conferences in Asia. These were held in the period October 1912 to May 1913. Their effect was to translate the hopes of Edinburgh into practical initiatives on the field.

They dealt specifically with issues such as the transfer of responsibility from foreign missionaries to emerging national leaders. Mott took the main responsibility for organising these events while Oldham launched the important journal, *The International Review of Mission*. Its first edition was published in January 1912 and it is still published today. The *Review* has had a major influence throughout the twentieth century in the furthering of an international and interdenominational debate on mission.

The Continuation Committee was intended to lead to the creation of a single, permanent representative body which would allow mission agencies throughout the world to communicate and co-operate with each other. In October 1921 such a body was created at a meeting convened in New York State. It was known as the International Missionary Council and it fulfilled the hopes of many for its work until it was finally merged with the World Council of Churches at the New Delhi Assembly in 1960.

Second, it is now clear that Edinburgh provided the impetus and practical framework that created the modern ecumenical movement.

The issue of bringing denominations in the West closer together was not really the purpose for which the Edinburgh Conference had been called. Indeed, those from an Anglo-Catholic background had only agreed to attend on the understanding that matters of faith and doctrine would not be on the agenda. Yet in discussing co-operation on the mission field, it was inevitable that the question of the export of the divisions of the West to the younger churches could hardly be avoided. Moreover, the spirit of unity which the delegates experienced created a desire for further discussions on the divided state of Christendom.

During the conference Bishop Brent of the Protestant Episcopal Church in the United States was inspired by a growing sense of the importance of a united church. He spoke of his vision while at Edinburgh and thereafter com-

mitted himself to working towards such an end. The movement which he became instrumental in promoting was known
as the Faith and Order Movement. It was the conferences of
this Movement, beginning in Lausanne in 1927 that lead
directly to the creation of the World Council of Churches
in 1948. The Faith and Order Movement developed in
parallel with the Life and Witness Movement, which,
although it predated the 1910 Edinburgh conference was
given added impetus by it. The Life and Witness Movement
was a further tributary that flowed into the growing ecumenical movement.

Third, although not discernible at the time, Edinburgh
1910 marked the point at which the initiative in mission
underwent a significant shift away from its evangelical
origins.

The reasons for this shift are complex and will be discussed in more detail in Chapter 5. For the moment it is
important to simply note that Edinburgh 1910 could not and
would not have taken place without a strong evangelical
enthusiasm both for mission and for unity amongst God's
people. Yet the decision, rightly taken, to include Christians
from other traditions coincided with a loss of nerve and
influence on the part of evangelicals. Institutions that they
had created and which had been important in making Edinburgh 1910 a reality gradually and increasingly moved away
from their evangelical origins.

Fourth, Edinburgh marked a decisive shift in the nature of
world mission.

The slogan of the Student Volunteer Movement, 'The
evangelization of the world in this generation', was brought
before the Edinburgh Conference by John Mott. Although
there was some debate about precisely what such a call really
meant, in large measure it was adopted by the Edinburgh
delegates as part of the event and in subsequent years has
been closely associated with Edinburgh 1910.[19] The hope
was not without foundation. A comparison of the relative

progress of the missionary movement between 1810 and 1910 suggested to the delegates that the completion of such a task was possible. It seemed to some that a combination of good methodology, adequate resources and full co-operation amongst Christians would enable the dream to be fulfilled. The Edinburgh Conference was specifically intended to produce such an outcome. But to a very large extent this call was seen as very much an Anglo-Saxon task. It was almost as if the responsibility to complete the Great Commission had fallen to the Anglo-Saxon peoples alone. Certainly the help of the young mission churches and national Christians would play a part, but the origin of the delegates at Edinburgh clearly demonstrated to many where the real initiative in missions lay. The world would be won for Christ from the secure mission base of Europe and North America. The twentieth-century reality in mission has been very different from such an expectation. In this sense Edinburgh 1910 did not so much presage what was to come in the new century as mark the end of the nineteenth century's approach to mission.

Notes

1. Adrian Hastings, *A History of English Christianity*, p. 34.
2. The precise reasons for the outbreak of revival in any setting are a matter of some debate. One strong argument suggests that new religious movments break out at times of great social change. This explanation would seem to help our understanding of some elements of revival during this period. However, it is possible to point to times of great social change without an accompanying revival and to revivals that do not seem to be occasioned by great social change. It is therefore unwise to think in terms of simple cause-and-effect solutions.
3. Derek Tidball, *Who are the Evangelicals?*, p. 33.
4. *Ibid.*, p. 35.
5. *Ibid.*, p. 40.
6. Adrian Hastings, *The World Mission of the Church*, pp. 38ff.

7. *Ibid.*, p.13.
8. Ruth Rouse and Stephen Neill (eds.), *A History of the Ecumenical Movement Vol. 1.*, p. 235.
9. Roland Allen, *The Spontaneous Expansion of the Church.*
10. Andrew Walls, St. Colm's Lecture, p. 13.
11. *The World Christian Encyclopedia*, edited by David Barrett, contains the following estimates for the percentages of Christians in the world:

    AD   500 22.4 per cent
    AD 1000 18.4 per cent
    AD 1500 19 per cent
    AD 1800 23.1 per cent

    The figure for 1800 represents some increase due to missionary activity.
12. R. Rouse, in *A History of the Ecumenical Movement Vol. 1.*, p. 309.
13. H. Brandreth, in *A History of the Ecumenical Movement Vol. 1.*, pp. 263ff.
14. R. Rouse, in *A History of the Ecumenical Movement Vol. 1.*, pp. 318ff.
15. K. Latourette, in *A History of the Ecumenical Movement*, p. 354.
16. See Alexander Boddy, *To Kai the Holy.*
17. K. Latourette, in *A History of the Ecumenical Movement Vol. 1.*, p. 354.
18. A. Walls, St. Colm's Lecture, p. 1.
19. See the discussion on this topic in S. Neill, *A History of Christian Missions*, p. 394.

CHAPTER THREE

FROM MISSION BASE TO MISSION FIELD

As the delegates at Edinburgh stood spontaneously at the end of the Conference to sing the doxology, and then streamed home to spread enthusiastic reports of all that had taken place, they could not have dreamt of the storm clouds that were to gather so quickly and so ominously in the few years following their departure. The outbreak of World War in 1914 dramatically altered many of the hopes so zealously expressed at Edinburgh. Andrew Walls puts it this way:

> The Edinburgh delegates could not have foreseen how many of their hopes for a speedy evangelization of the world through missionary mobilisation would drain away into the trenches of France and Flanders, or how, within a few short years, a World War would make many schemes of international co-operation seem laughable. The Atlantic prosperity that had underwritten the missionary movement went into crisis, and economic depression eroded its financial basis as the war had reduced its manpower base.[1]

The killing fields of Flanders

But the effect of the First World War was not just to diminish manpower and resources for overseas mission, though this certainly did happen. Much more seriously, the First World War made a profound impression on Christian Europe itself. It is perhaps hard for those of us who live at the end of the

twentieth century and who were born after the chilling reality
of two World Wars to understand the implications of those
two wars for the civilian populations of Europe. War is never
pleasant, especially for those caught up in the immediate
violence of the conflict. But for the first time in human
history, war in the twentieth century touched and involved
the civilian population in a way that earlier wars never had.
The concept of total war, where the whole industrial, economic, political, social and military resources of a nation are
absolutely committed to the war effort, is relatively new. In
such a situation the civilian population is involved in the
conflict in a much more direct fashion.

Certainly the First and Second World Wars, albeit in rather
different ways, touched the psyche of the nationals of Europe
in a very profound manner. It is clear that church attendance
in Europe began to decrease following the outbreak of the
First World War. To some extent there was a direct relationship between the War and subsequent losses in attendance
and then in membership. The conflict involved many millions of men who became displaced from their normal
occupations and places of worship. It was hard for many to
resume the normal routine of family and church life once the
war was ended. Many of those men who returned did not
return to church worship. Their wives might have continued
and they may well have sent their children to Sunday School
but the lack of active involvement of the fathers in families
eventually took its toll.

While it is true that the First World War brought some to a
living faith and strengthened the faith of others, it is also the
case that many men were completely sickened by what they
saw and lost their faith completely. Even for those who
returned without becoming ardent atheists life could never
be the same again. The churches, the bishops, archbishops
and cardinals of Europe had all urged their compatriots to
take up arms against the enemies of their respective countries. All had claimed that God was on their side. Their army

chaplains had reinforced the message of the bishops and other church leaders. The author A. J. Cronin, writing a fictional work in 1941, caught something of this mood when he commented somewhat prophetically through the words of one of his characters:

> The church will suffer for its cowardice. A viper nourished in one's bosom will one day strike that bosom. To sanction the might of arms is to invite destruction. The day may come when great military forces will break loose and turn upon the Church, corrupting millions of her children, sending her down again — a timid shadow — into the Catacombs.[2]

The combination of long years of war, the knowledge that the churches had somehow sanctioned the conflict, the realisation that it was primarily the ancient Christian nations of Europe that were killing one another and the rather direct involvement of whole civilian populations seemed to change the whole perspective of Europe concerning the hope, or lack of it, that Christianity offered. As Hastings puts it:

> The 1914 war had appeared as fruit of the traditional and Christian order of Europe. Clerics had whipped up enthusiasm for it in the earlier stages and the profound disillusionment that followed had been with religion as much as with anything else.[3]

Certainly the response of Europeans to Christianity following both the First and Second World Wars stood in marked contrast to the experience of Christianity in those nations which had had some involvement in the War but for whom it was a distant experience, most notably the United States. Far from the two World Wars damaging church life in America, statistics suggest positive growth in the immediate post-war years. However, social dislocation of a very different kind was beginning to impact American church life. In the nineteenth century, and especially in the latter half of that century, it was clearly evangelical, revivalist, white Protestantism that dominated both church and public life. Whereas some of the early American Presidents, such as Jefferson, had tended towards Deism, the American Presidents of the latter years of the nineteenth century were much more evangelical and orthodox in their outlook. The heartland of this Protestant religious force was that of small town and rural America. These were the communities that set the political, social and religious agenda for the nation.

By the post-war years this Protestant hegemony was beginning to be challenged. One statistic illustrates the process well. In 1870 less than ten million Americans (26 per cent of the population) lived in towns of 2500 or more. By 1930 nearly 70 million (56 per cent of the population) lived in such communities.[4] This did not shake the confidence of the church at first, but it was becoming much more difficult for the former Protestant consensus to place its stamp on the nation's priorities. Although not to the same extent as in Europe, within forty years of Edinburgh 1910 the confidence of the church, so evident as the new century had dawned, was beginning to be questioned.

But the European experience of war, powerful and formative as it proved to be, was not the only factor at work in eroding the mission base in Europe.

Losing the base

In surveying their prospects for the coming twentieth century, the churches had exhibited one very painful blindspot. Their hopeful prognosis for future days had taken little account of the long-standing alienation of the working classes from the church. There had been many prophets who had pointed out the existence of this gulf. A number of movements in the latter half of the nineteenth century had particularly attempted to address this problem. In England, there was the work of the Salvation Army on one wing of the church, and that of many Anglo-Catholic priests who dedicated themselves to the working-class poor, on an opposite wing of the church. These and other initiatives attempted to address the problem, but problem there was.

In England, part of the problem lay in the social stratification of the denominations. The Free Churches had often begun amongst the working classes and lower middle classes but for the most part those that had joined the Free Churches were often those who were what we might call the aspiring working class. They had ambitions to improve themselves. Indeed some Free Churches in the nineteenth century and well into the twentieth century had what were called 'Improvement Classes'. The phenomenon which we know as 'redemption and lift' was almost an intrinsic part of Free Church culture. The work ethic, the emphasis on thrift, on abstinence from alcohol and tobacco, the importance placed on education together with opportunities to exercise leadership were all part of this process of social movement up and away from working-class roots. The grandchildren of converted miners and millworkers became doctors, lawyers, teachers, politicians; professionals of every kind.

The Church of England was very much the church of the better-off middle classes. Certainly some working-class people attended Anglican churches. Some writers have described the loyal Anglican working class as coming close to the stereotypical Tory working class — the compliant working classes.

It was of course true that the Roman Catholic church had retained the loyalty of many working-class people. Indeed, in many English cities, Roman Catholic congregations were almost entirely working class in their composition. But where this was true, it was almost entirely an immigrant Irish working class. The older and existing English membership of the Roman Catholic church was almost entirely drawn from the upper classes. It was not the English working classes that attended Catholic churches.

There is some debate as to precisely when this alienation of the working classes from the church began. The discussion is not unimportant since the answer one gives to the question implies an analysis as to the nature of the problem itself. Some maintain that the alienation began at the time of industrialisation, suggesting that in the rural idyll religion thrived amongst the working classes. Others have cast great doubt on this scenario, suggesting instead that working-class allegiance to the church was always less complete than the picture painted by popular imagination.[5] Still others argue that even when the working classes were present in church the religion they espoused owed more to a Christianised paganism than it did to a biblical Christianity.[6] Whatever the precise point at which such alienation began and whatever the precise cause, we can say with some confidence that it is one which is both long-standing and deep.

Nor is the phenomenon of the isolation of generations of working people from the church unique to England. Other parts of Europe have also felt the problem acutely. Perhaps the best-documented account of working-class deChristianisation is in France. Although some lone voices had pointed to the problem of what was spoken of as 'a wall between the church and the working class' ever since the final decades of the nineteenth century, the one study that finally shook the French church was a detailed work entitled *France, pays de mission?*, published in 1943. Although not a literal translation, perhaps the best English rendering of this title would be *France: a mission field?*

The data contained in this study were sufficiently detailed to convince any who doubted that the church had long been deserted by the working class of France. But the most helpful aspect of the work was not this statistical analysis, so much as the assertion that what was needed was not an improvement of the parish system, more resources, more priests, better methods and so on. Instead, it argued that since France must now be regarded as a mission field, a totally new approach needed to be adopted. Not a better-organised church but a different church; a mission church. The idea that any country in Europe represented a mission field came as an appalling shock to many. Could it be possible that the secure mission base of thirty years ago, the inheritor of possibly fifteen hundred years of Christian witness, had itself become the mission field?[7]

Yet the realisation that Europe had become just that, a mission field, was burningly apparent to those who came to that continent from other lands. By the end of the Second World War, the alienation of the working classes, so complete in places, was matched by what Hastings calls the 'agnostic consensus' of the leaders of Europe. These men knew, understood and valued Europe's Christian heritage. They saw how it differed dramatically from the ideology of Fascism but their personal belief and commitment was half-hearted indeed. One Christian leader from South Africa who had been moved by the suffering in Europe following the Second World War, came to live and work in Europe. He wrote to a close friend:

> I have been very busy since I arrived here. The few days in England, Belgium and Holland were a great blessing to my soul and it was good to get some firsthand knowledge of the work. However, during the last few weeks I have learnt a lot about the situation in Europe and I am deeply burdened with the appalling darkness in the spiritual life of these nations. The physical suffering because of the lack of food and clothes is a detail in comparison with the spiritual need and suffering.[8]

The same leader wrote almost incredulously in a newsletter sent to supporters and friends around the world:

> . . . the writer never realised this until he came here and possibly millions do not realise the heathen state of the people of Europe. Here are 400,000,000 precious souls that have never handled a Bible and that do not know that Jesus is the Saviour of mankind. Here we met with educated, civilised, white heathen.[9]

Competing ideologies

However dramatic the impact of two World Wars on the soul of Europe, these events are not enough to explain the unexpected decline of Christianity in Europe during the twentieth century. Nor do the divisions and failures of the church, serious as they might be, account by themselves for the increasing marginalisation of the church throughout the twentieth century. Just as important, if not more so, had been the sense that other competing and powerful secular ideologies have taken centre stage during the greater part of the period since the outbreak of the First World War. Just as the nineteenth century was strongly influenced by a Christian faith infused with the evangelical momentum of a previous century, so the intellectual and popular ideas that influenced the whole century also depend crucially on key developments from an earlier age. The last half of the nineteenth century saw the emergence of an increasingly secular ideology which drew heavily on a diverse combination of new intellectual claims, for example, the social and political analyses of Marx, the philosophical radicalism of Nietzsche, the psychology of Freud and the biology of Darwin.[10] Elements from the work of these men, and from others, began to be used to construct a secular explanation of the story of the world and of man's place in it. Whereas the Christian story begins with the creation and the subsequent fall of man, so that in one sense mankind is seen as always living to some extent in the shadow of that fall, the new secular story saw the past as imperfect not because of a mythic 'fall' but only because of a lack of knowledge. Man was moving ever more into the secular light. To put it at its most basic, the Christian story of mankind is partly that of the descent of man, the secular story of man is of his ascent.

The utopian dream of the secular myth no longer looks for the return of the Messiah in order for the kingdom of God to be established. The glorious city of Christian apocalyptic hope, the new Jerusalem, will be built now. The great tool of man's ascent is that of science with its accompanying technology. The great liberation of man is the realisation that religion is mere superstition and can now be dispensed with. Reason and education will bring civilisation and hence happiness to all. As nations become more enlightened wars will cease, hunger and other human needs will be overcome in the context of man's fraternity.

Standing as we do at the end of a century which has felt the impact of those who have believed such secular fairy stories such pronouncements seem fantastic, yet even now there are many for whom such thinking forms an important part of their unconscious world view. Another descriptive term for such views is the term 'scientism'. Such scientism is still deeply imbedded in much popular thinking and indeed in the views of leading thinkers even at the end of the twentieth century. For them:

> Man stands at the centre of a universe in which he is autonomous. He is an orphan in the universe but an orphan so powerful that he can be supremely optimistic about his standing and status in the world. The processes by which the universe works are in principle understandable and, to quote Stephen Hawking, once we do understand them all, 'we will know the mind of God', not because we will have found God but because man will finally stand in the place of God.[11]

The issue of power stands at the centre of those twentieth-century ideologies which have used the mythology of scientism and the 'inevitability' of progress to give their systems a pseudo-scientific basis. Three systems have had a profound effect on the lives (and deaths) of millions of people who have lived in the West during the twentieth century.

1. International communism

Standing as we do on this side of the fall of the Berlin Wall, it hardly seems possible to talk of the power of communism as an alternative ideology. Yet, if we survey the whole of the twentieth-century history in Europe, communism stands as a vitally important force that has shaped the experience of several generations. It is not merely that Communist governments dominated large parts of Europe for at least half a century; countries which had formerly been influenced by the culture of Christianity: it is also the case that the influence of a socialist ideology has reached well beyond the boundaries of Soviet hegemony.

In the 1920s it was notable how many younger intellectuals in many Western countries looked with admiration to the Russia of Stalin. The following decade brought with it the fight against fascism, notably in Spain. Many young men from a whole range of European countries volunteered to fight against the forces of Franco. They were by no means a majority of their generation, nor were they even necessarily representative of it, and yet somehow they did represent the increasing leftwards movement of much political thought in Europe. Economics became dominated by the interventionist thinking of Keynes. Social planning in the field of housing and health, the nationalisation of key industries; these and other developments heralded a shift in the social and political consensus of society. This broad popular shift in Europe led to the surprise defeat of a Conservative Winston Churchhill at the British General Election of 1945. Despite the years of Conservative government in Britain during the 1950s, there was little talk of reversing nationalisation or socialised medicine.

By the 1960s some political commentators were speaking of future Communist governments in Italy and France, of a socialist future for Germany and of a demographic shift in British political life that would ensure that the Conservatives would never enter office again. During the 1960s Conservative students were an endangered species on British university campuses. Those that did exist sounded more like moderate socialists. The Communist government of Mao

Zedong (Tse-Tung) commanded the same place in the minds of radical students that Stalin's Russia had enjoyed among some intellectuals in earlier decades.

Even in the United States, where communism was never likely to gain any popular acceptance as a political ideology, commentators have argued that the interventionism of Roosevelt's 'New Deal' in the 1930s and the actual scale of Federal spending in the economy during the decades since suggests that the place of government in determining the shape of society has undergone a decisive shift from that of an earlier century. The notion that you become what you bitterly oppose is not always so far from the truth. The fact that communism as an ideology and as a system of government has been demonstrated to have failed does not mean that many of the underlying assumptions of such a system have not percolated deeply into the consciousness of modern man.

2. Fascism as secular paganism

Clearly, fascism as a functioning political force has been utterly discredited by its particular manifestation in the Third Reich. But there is a tendency to forget that Franco's Spain and an equally right-wing government in Portugal survived almost as long as many of the Communist regimes of Eastern Europe. Fascism draws deeply from the well of nationalism and religious feeling. Even in its extreme Nazi form, it is salutary to remember the large number of those in the educated elite of Western lands who were influenced significantly by the dark prejudices of fascist thought. Especially by its use of disciplines such as genetics, Nazi ideology claimed to have a strongly scientific base.

The roots of Nazi thinking in Nietzsche are now very clear.[12] While the precise forms of fascist political organisation are both suppressed and carefully monitored it is increasingly obvious that the basic wellsprings that enabled fascism to emerge so quickly and so powerfully have not disappeared. It is not only a frustrated and racist form of nationalism that still waits to ambush the nations of Europe. The power of a strongly man-centred and pagan encounter with our world constitutes a continuing theme in modern European culture. A number of writers including Paul Tillich have demonstrated very persuasively that fascism is but one manifestation of a widespread neo-paganism that makes itself felt in a variety of forms. As Visser't Hooft says:

> Nietzsche has become again a favoured guide. And the lay preachers of paganism, in the period between the world wars, D. H. Lawrence and Hermann Hesse, are more widely read than ever before. Lawrence, whom F. R. Leavis calls 'still the great writer of our own phase of civilization', has consistently sought to replace Christianity by a life-affirming or, as he called it, 'dark religion'.[13]

During the twentieth century it has been tempting for those who recognise the religious dimensions in both fascism and other forms of neo-paganism to attempt to produce an alliance between Christianity and these other religious forces. Such a marriage will always and inevitably be an unholy and dangerous alliance.

3. Western liberal capitalism

It is much easier for those of us who live in Western Europe or in North America to detect the flaws in communism or in fascism than it is for us to comment on the system which dominates our own societies. Some would almost certainly want to claim that our societies are not dominated by a particular ideology. In the West we live in a free and open society and are able to choose to adopt any or no ideology. As we look at ourselves and our neighbours we may well be tempted to think that the majority in our society have taken the option of adopting no ideology at all. Such a conclusion would be a self-deception. The collapse of communism was seen very clearly by the political leaders of the West as the triumph of one system over another. Fukuyama's book *The End of History* took as its major theme the notion that up until now modern history has consisted of the competition of one major ideological system with another. Therefore, in one sense, the triumph of liberal capitalism ends history as we have known it.

Those who have been on the receiving end of the victory of the West over the communism of Eastern Europe are also under no illusion that liberal capitalism consists of a very clear ideology and not merely the absence of ideology. Many societies in Eastern Europe have been shaken by the impact of Western consumerism. They are struck by the ability of capitalism to supply goods and services but equally shocked by the apparent absence of any moral basis for such a system. The obvious immorality of a communist system built on deceit is now simply replaced by a system which seems to be more efficient, but which accompanies that efficiency with an amorality that is socially devastating.

What kind of ideology is it that takes such an amoral stance? The older forms of capitalism were moderated to a considerable degree by the inheritance of a Christian past which, some argue, acted as the very inspiration for capitalism itself. However, in recent years, the necessary connection with a Christian understanding of morality has been cut, and replaced with what is sometimes thought of as a kind of social and economic Darwinism, even though Darwin himself never advocated such an agenda. The older utopian secular humanism has learnt the lessons of the twentieth century concerning the inhumanity of mankind. The idea that the greater good of society will always emerge as mankind gains more knowledge has been significantly modified in the late twentieth century. The idea that it is the fittest who will survive, both in biological and economic terms, has been interpreted as a moral principle, namely the fittest deserve to survive. The role of the state has increasingly changed from being the instrument which will allow society to usher in the new Utopia to one in which the state merely ameliorates the worst excesses of a society where the fittest gain the greatest rewards. The hidden forces of the market are thought to be so powerful that even the most powerful of states cannot withstand them. Only the recognition of how these hidden forces operate and the adjustment of our society to co-operate with them can bring the greatest good to the greatest number of people.

A vision of society

The underlying theme of any ideology offers a particular vision of society and of an individual's relationship to that society. The leaders of the evangelical Christian cause in the nineteenth century had a clear vision of society. That vision began with the conviction that the character of mankind had been fatally flawed by the fall of man but that the life of Jesus Christ offered the opportunity for a new beginning. The church was God's instrument to bring the life-giving message to the world. Even though God's ultimate intention for the reconciliation of the created order to his entire purpose could not be fulfilled completely in this life, nevertheless a great deal could be accomplished by redeemed men and women living in the light of the revelation brought by Jesus Christ. The motivation produced by the desire to apply the love of God to the structures of society produced a reforming zeal in much nineteenth-century Christianity. Even though Christians did not always agree on the detail of a political application of such reform, the rightness of such efforts was rarely doubted. Commenting on the position of Christianity in late nineteenth-century America, Mark Noll says:

> In general, Protestants in the nation's Progressive Era had few difficulties in translating their beliefs in the saving power of Christ and the authority of the Bible into an intuitive but none-theless powerful political attitude. Most saw reform at home as the natural complement to missionary activity overseas.[14]

But even though a few notable individuals have held such convictions in the twentieth century, in general, the confidence of nineteenth-century Christianity's vision of society has been noticeably less compelling as Christianity faced the competing ideologies of the twentieth century. Those individuals with strong Christian convictions were much more likely to interpret their hopes in the context of other ideologies — a Christian socialism or a Christian view of liberal capitalism. While institutions such as the British Labour Party maintained their Christian roots such an interpretation was not too problematic, but as the twentieth century progressed it became increasingly difficult for Christians to hold to a distinctive Christian social and political agenda. The tendency in the Western world has been for Christians either to adopt a highly individualistic personal morality which has been increasingly unconnected to a wider vision for society, or to become rather reactionary in their stance. In short, it has been easier for Christians to indicate what they are against rather than what they are for.

In this sense, a Christian vision for society has tended to be seen as essentially looking to the past; as something that attempts to preserve a past that has disappeared altogether. Visions of a brave new world in the twentieth century have tended to be inspired by an essentially secular viewpoint with Christianity appearing only at the margins. Even though secular hopes have often proved to be false, a clear Christian alternative has not figured in the thinking of twentieth-century Western society. Whereas medieval society could be inspired by books such as *The Imitation of Christ*, the closing decade of the twentieth century is much more likely to be inspired by the more temporal vision of the imitation of Richard Branson.

The continuing absence of a convincing Christian vision for society and the awareness that more recent Western alternatives have also proved wanting has produced something of an abyss for the culture of the West. The option of a highly individualistic neo-paganism has remained as an important subculture in society. Some have seen the emergence of a variety of pagan worship practices, including the overtly occult, and of a range of so-called New Age religious systems as expressions of that powerful undercurrent. Still others are beginning to look to older religious systems that come from totally outside the West for a vision of society.

The challenge of other faiths

The Edinburgh delegates were concerned to take the good news of Jesus Christ to the non-Christian world. They perceived a clear distinction between Christendom (largely the nations of the West) and 'Heathendom'. They differed a little in their attitude towards other religions but not fundamentally so. As Stephen Neill puts it:

> . . . all were agreed that, as the Lordship of Christ came to be recognised, these other religions would disappear in their present form — the time would come when Siva and Vishnu would have no more worshippers than Zeus and Apollo have today. Expression of these views might differ a little in detail; it cannot be questioned that in 1910 there was practical unanimity with regard to the substance of them.[15]

The experience of the twentieth century has demonstrated that the other major world religions have not just disappeared as the Christian gospel has been proclaimed. On the contrary, Buddhism, Hinduism and Islam have all undergone an unexpected renewal during the past eighty years. In part this renewal has itself been a reaction to the missionary activity of Christianity. To some extent there has come an identification of religion with the emerging nationalism that has been such a feature of the anti-colonial and now post-colonial experience of the second half of the twentieth century. Although many liberation movements were inspired initially by secular ideologies, particularly by socialism, that phase has now developed into a nationalism that is imbued with traditional religious expression. So the socialism of Gaddafi has become the Green revolution of Islam much more than the Red revolution of socialism. The secular state of India has been identified increasingly with the idea that to be truly Indian is to be Hindu. The anti-colonial and anti-Western rhetoric of Islam in Africa has suggested that Christianity is inevitably the religion of colonialism and repression and that Islam is the ancient expression of what it means to be an African.

At an even more fundamental level, Christian missionary activity has inspired other religions to engage in a degree of internal reform. In India, Hinduism has learnt from Christianity something of what it means to be concerned for social reform. Islam, troubled for many years by the success of the Christian West in terms of economic and military might, has seen the ending of colonialism and the wealth that has come from oil as indicating the strength of Islam. A new apologetic for Islam has been forged on the basis of contact with the Christian West, especially in the light of what it sees as Western (and so Christian) decadence.

Beyond a revitalised faith in the traditional areas of strength for Islam, Hinduism and Buddhism, all three of these faiths have observed closely the missionary methods of Christianity and have sought in a variety of ways to use the same methods in missionary activity in the West. Whereas the delegates at Edinburgh might have been able to foresee a strengthening of these older religions in their traditional homelands, the idea that within forty years of Edinburgh these same religions would be present as missionaries in the West would have been unimaginable. Yet that is what has taken place. As the twentieth century comes to a close, not only is the mission base now a mission field for Christianity, it is a mission field in which Christianity is in significant competition with the very faiths that the Edinburgh delegates dedicated themselves to winning for Christ in distant lands.

Notes

1. Andrew Walls, St. Colm's lecture, p. 2.
2. A. J. Cronin, *The Keys of the Kingdom*, p. 215.
3. Adrian Hastings, *A History of English Christianity*, p. 383.
4. Mark Noll, *A History of Christianity in the United States and Canada*, p. 364.
5. Martin Robinson, *Celebrating the Small Church*, pp. 42ff.
6. The case that Europe was only ever superficially converted from paganism is argued in Anton Wessels, *Europe: Was it Ever Really Christian?*
7. Oscar Amal, *Priests in Working-Class Blue*, pp. 53ff.
8. Letter from David du Plessis to Robert McGlasson, 22 January 1948, quoted in M. Robinson, *To the Ends of the Earth*, p. 115.
9. Newsletter from David du Plessis, *Come . . . Inherit*, p. 2 quoted in M. Robinson, *To the Ends of the Earth*, p. 115.
10. Martin Robinson, *The Faith of the Unbeliever*, pp. 40ff.
11. *Ibid.*, Chap 2.
12. David Burnett makes it clear that Hitler was much more influenced by the explicitly occult than by Nietzsche. See *Dawning of the Pagan Moon*.
13. Visser't Hooft, *International Review of Mission*, January 1974, pp. 353ff.
14. Mark Noll, *op. cit.*, pp. 299ff.
15. Stephen Neill, *op. cit.*, pp. 454ff.

CHAPTER FOUR

THE CHURCH MOVES SOUTH

The aspiration of the delegates at Edinburgh 1910 was to see the gospel proclaimed to all nations in their generation. They saw Europe and North America as the strong sending base that would accomplish this task. The 1914–1918 conflict in Europe robbed the international missionary cause of much-needed resources, both financial and human. But the conflict also marked a deep change in the course of the missionary movement in quite unforeseen ways. At a fairly superficial level, Germany's losing of the war caused the particular missions that they had supported to undergo significant change. Some of these missions were in parts of Africa where the territory passed to the Allies as part of the war settlement. The shift in colonial oversight brought inevitable change to the work of local missions in those areas. Initially there had been a proposal that all German property, including the property of missions, should be passed to the allied governments. Fortunately, British and American Christians, largely through the International Missionary Council, were able to prevent this happening, but these problems underlined an essential difficulty. The blunt truth was that Western missions had become too dependent on Western colonialism. Though few could see it at the time, the 1914–1918 conflict was the beginning of the end for colonialism.

The colonial connection

The simplistic accusation of some critics of Christianity is that colonialism and Christian missions were interchangeable and mutually dependent movements. The idea that lies behind such an accusation is that early explorers were followed by isolated traders, and that once the way was opened up by such as these, missionaries followed to 'tame' the natives. Colonial power then followed which was used to reinforce the position of both traders and missionaries. Case histories from early Roman Catholic missions in Japan, together with reference to pioneers such as David Livingstone, are often cited in support of such claims. The reality is much more complex.

Certainly there are many instances when missionaries opened up extensive fields long before there was any colonial power present. There are well-documented cases of missionaries acting almost as emissaries for their own government as well as for the cause of Christ. Max Warren quotes from a letter outlining the duties of a lay missionary working for the Church Missionary Society amongst the Yoruba people in 1853, before foreign rule. The letter suggested that his duties should include being:

> . . . a counsellor of the chiefs in respect of military policy and warfare. You will be able to advise them in the best way of fortifying their town, and of securing their territory from sudden attack, and at the same time dissuade them from all aggressive warfare . . . Another department of your office will be to communicate with the vice-consul and consul and with the officers of the squadron upon the affairs of the tribe . . . We look forward to some recognition of your position by Her Majesty's government, which may give you an advantage in conducting such communications beyond that which you might have as an agent of the Society.[1]

The intrinsic relationship between imperialism and mission was well stated by Lord Rosebury in 1895:

> Liberal imperialism implies, first, the maintenance of the Empire; secondly, the opening up of new areas for our surplus population; thirdly the suppression of the slave trade; fourthly, the development of missionary enterprise; and fifthly the development of our commerce, which so often needs it.[2]

The closeness of this relationship is well demonstrated by the fact that, at least up until 1914, national missionaries tended only to work in those countries in which their own nation was the predominant power. But in two important respects, the apparent interconnectedness between mission and imperialism did not work at all. First, there are certainly a number of examples when the presence of missionaries did not at all suit the colonial power. Although the flag frequently followed the Bible, it was not always the case that the Bible followed the flag.

Second, and more importantly, there is good evidence that the missionary movement acted as the 'mother of African nationalism' and indeed of a good many other anti-colonial movements. The case is easier to demonstrate in Africa and is put very persuasively by the African nationalist Sithole, in his book *African Nationalism*.[3] The process by which the missionary movement aided the movement towards nationalism is a complex matter. At one level the relationship is very simple, namely, the overwhelming majority of the leaders of African nationalism were educated in mission schools. It was their access to a Western form of education that gave such leaders the tools with which to combat colonialism. Church life often added to the skills gained in schools by offering avenues for leadership which might otherwise not have been available to emerging national leaders. But at a much deeper level, there is an inherent impetus because of the content of the gospel message itself, which impelled those who heard its message to live and work for freedom. In just the same way that the early missionary movement worked to eradicate slavery and other social ills, so national Christians could sense that the structures of colonial and imperial life could, ultimately, never survive the scrutiny of gospel. Even though missionaries didn't always realise it, theirs was a deeply subversive message.

Clearly, the preaching of the gospel was only one factor in producing a strong movement towards the ending of colonial rule during the inter-war years. Some have mistakenly thought that the Second World War was the decisive factor in signalling the end of Empire but it is much more likely that it only hastened the inevitable. European minds might not have seen it but in fact most nationalist movements had begun in some earnest before the Second World War broke out.

The end of the colonial period induced a sense of foreboding amongst some missionaries. Many were convinced that the end of colonial rule and the patronage that went with it would severely hamper the work of mission. Nor was it just the missionaries who felt that the advancing tide of nationalism and the end of imperialism would strike a fatal blow at Christian mission. Stephen Neill quotes the Indian diplomat and historian, K. M. Pannikkar as making the same case. Neill summarised Pannikar's argument as follows:

> . . . Christian missionary work in Asia is merely an epiphenomenon of Western political and economic expansion. Now that the West is everywhere politically in retreat, the diminution of its missionary effort, and consequently of Christian influence in Asian affairs, is to be expected.[4]

Many missionaries were afraid that Pannikar and other similar prophets of doom were right. They feared that national leaders were not yet ready to take on the burden of leadership, and that once missionaries were withdrawn the young churches on the mission field would flounder and fail. They could not see how the vast institutions, hospitals and schools, could be maintained without missionary staff and missionary money. Worse still, they believed that where such institutions were taken over by newly independent nations that the loss of these facilities would deprive the Christian cause of much-needed influence in the societies where they were situated.

Other factors added to the gloomy prognosis. Some were aware that missionaries were not only likely to be unwelcome in some lands, they would be actively barred from entering others. Only colonial patronage had allowed the gospel to be preached at all in some Muslim nations. The end of Empire in these places would mean the end of Christian witness. They were aware that some national leaders actively encouraged the return of older indigenous tribal religions as part of the expression of nationalism. Could it be that the end of the colonial period would actually sweep away all of the gains of the missionary movement to date?

This lack of confidence about the future of the tender shoots of Christian witness was reinforced by a growing questioning about the goals of mission. Many of the major mission agencies were no longer so sure that missions should be emphasising evangelism and the establishing of the church so much as working in the field of social and economic development. The debate which could be polarised along the theme of 'tracts or tractors' was affecting mission thinking more and more.[5]

Finally, some were aware that demographic trends did not favour the growth of the church. The bald fact was that population growth in the traditional Christian heartlands of Europe and North America had slowed considerably. At the same time, some of the fastest population growth in the world was taking place in precisely those countries where Christian witness was at its weakest. The combination of all these factors led one population expert working for the World Council of Churches to make this forecast in 1968:

Towards the end of this century, Christians will comprise no more than eight per cent of the world's population — assuming that present demographic growth will not be arrested in some unforeseen manner . . . Even the best missionary strategy with a conventional approach to the field of church planting and church growth will have no material effect upon this prognosis.[6]

Given that Christianity had begun the century comprising some 33 per cent of the world's population, this would seem to represent a major reverse for the hopes of the Edinburgh delegates in 1910. Enough time has now elapsed since 1968 for us to know that something unexpected has indeed happened. In the years since that prediction was made, there has come a very slight dip in the percentage of the world that claims to be Christian, but since that time, the figures have started to grow again. It is now predicted that the actual figure will be 35 per cent at the end of this century and could be as high as 40 per cent by the year 2050. To quote the editors of *Earthen Vessels*:

> Contrary to prevailing impressions, the days of the missionary are far from over. While missions historian Kenneth Scott Latourette called the nineteenth century the 'great century' of Christianity's expansion, the twentieth century has witnessed an even more astonishing growth of the Christian faith as a world religion. More people are coming to profess faith now than ever before.[7]

Enter the unexpected!

Given the demographic trends recognised so correctly in 1968, the only way in which it would have been possible to maintain the percentage of Christians in relation to the world's population explosion is for extensive and unprecedented conversion growth to have taken place in the final third of the twentieth century. This is indeed what seems to have taken place. Five largely unforeseen factors have contributed to this unexpected development.

1. Effective leadership by nationals

First, the national leadership of the younger national churches has been far more effective at leading their churches than foreign missionaries expected. Why should this be? Jonathan Bonk has documented in some detail the blinding effect that the relative wealth of missionaries has when they consider the role and contribution of nationals. He cites the story of one Indonesian church leader responding to a conference theme which bore the title, *Partnership in obedience*. 'Yes,' retorts the Indonesian brother, 'partnership for you, obedience for us.'[8]

The tendency of national Christians faced with the overwhelming powerful superiority which is built into the missionary/national relationship is either to stay silent and hence to be ineffective, or to speak out and be faced with the probability of isolation. Many of the most effective national leaders did not stay silent and so were often lost to the mission church. Even those who managed to stay did not always have their ability recognised by the foreign missionary. While missionaries were in power there was often a tendency to promote compliant nationals to leadership positions. No wonder the foreign missionary came to the conclusion that the national leadership was not yet ready to carry responsibility. Those who are willing to be compliant are rarely the leaders that you require! The post-colonial situation often forced missionaries to withdraw before they were ready to do so. It was not unusual for leaders to emerge after the missionaries had departed whom the missionaries themselves would never have appointed.

An early indication of the hidden leadership potential of national Christians can be found in the records of the Baptist Missionary Society in a survey of the position in the Indian State of Orissa during the period 1932–1933. The lack of funds occasioned by the economic collapse in Britain during the depression had forced the withdrawal of many missionaries. The result was that the church grew significantly as national Christians took leadership responsibility. Commenting on these figures the British author of the report stated: 'A wrong inference from the figures I have just quoted would be this — a decrease in the number of missionaries leads to an increase of strength to the Church and to increased giving.'[9]

Evidence from a later period would suggest that far from being a wrong inference it is a very correct one! As early as 1927 Roland Allen wrote passionately of the essential conflict produced by the expressed desire of missionaries to 'work themselves out of a job' — to see national Christians trained and carrying the leadership load — and the reality, which is that missionaries have far too often found every reason for not releasing responsibility to national Christians.[10] Is it possible that the enforced withdrawal of missionaries because of the national sensitivities of newly independent nations should be seen as part of God's strategy for the growth of the church?

This is not to argue that there is no role for the foreign missionary. Lamin Sanneh argues for the continued engagement of Western missionaries in Africa but makes the important qualification that it will in future necessitate a different kind of relationship. The role suggested by Sanneh is one of support, but as directed by national Christian leadership.[11]

2. Independent national churches

Second, the growth of the church in many parts of the world has been utterly transformed by the creation of churches independent of any missionary control. As you might expect, for many years foreign missionaries were inclined either to dismiss these new churches as unimportant or to see them as in some sense sub-Christian, or as examples of syncretism. But the continuing story of these churches indicates that the great majority are authentically Christian in their belief and practice.

During the first multiracial elections in South Africa, observant viewers would have noticed that all of the political party leaders, including Mandela and De Clerk, attended the annual convention of one particular church. Small wonder that they did so, because its membership is in the millions. It is the largest denomination in South Africa by far, and it is an independent African church. Even though the greatest impact of independent churches around the world has been felt in the last third of the twentieth century, such churches began to come into being very early in the twentieth century and even in some cases in the later years of the nineteenth century.

As you might expect, the origins of such churches are very varied. In the case of some churches, especially in Southern Africa, where the problem of white racism was present from an early time, many African leaders simply refused to remain any longer under white leadership and separated themselves and their followers from the white-led mission churches. In his classic study of what he calls 'Bantu Prophets', Bengt Sundkler identifies two main types of African independent churches. The first he calls 'Ethiopian Churches', and the second 'Zionist Churches'.[12] The term 'Ethiopian' does not suggest any contact with the country of that name but rather with the use of the term as an older name for the whole of Africa. In a similar way, the designation 'Zion' has no connection with any location in Israel but instead stands for a particular vision of the church. It is a strongly 'charismatic' vision of the Christian community, though it predates the outbreak of the Pentecostal movement itself.

Other independent churches grew up around the ministry of individuals who did not aspire to any leadership role within existing white-led missions. One example of this type of church can be found in the country of Zaire. It is an entirely black-led, African church which began through the vision of one man, Simon Kimbangu in Zaire (formerly the Belgian Congo). Kimbangu (known as a prophet by his followers) was baptised as a Baptist in 1915. His public ministry began in 1921 with the healing of one particular woman. News of this and other healings spread rapidly and Kimbangu unexpectedly found himself leading a vibrant movement. It did not take long for the colonial authority to begin to clamp down on his activities and there began a period of severe persecution. After only five months of public ministry, Kimbangu was arrested and sentenced to 120 lashes to be followed by execution. Through the intervention of some missionaries, the sentence was reduced by the Belgian King to life imprisonment. Kimbangu was deported to Katanga and died in prison there thirty years later.

His followers were also persecuted. Despite this, Kimbanguist congregations were secretly organised in the former Belgian Congo (Zaire), the French Congo, Gabon, Angola and Ruanda. It is estimated that some 37,000 heads of families were deported for being Kimbanguists. It is claimed that simply to utter the name of Simon Kimbangu was enough to bring deportation without trial. Most of those who were deported died in exile.

For nearly forty years this persecution continued until the Kimbanguists themselves decided to act in a very public protest. In 1957, some 600 leading Kimbanguists sent a letter of petition to the Belgian Governor, General Petillon. The letter asked the governor for religious liberty and told him that all of those who petitioned him would assemble in a particular sports stadium: 'There you can kill us if you want to.' The Kimbanguists were asking for death or liberty. This action was the beginning of liberty and by 1959 the Church of the Prophet Simon Kimbangu was officially recognised by the Belgian authorities. In 1969 the Kimbanguists were admitted into membership of the World Council of Churches as a recognised Christian denomination. Today the church has many millions of members and is arguably the largest Protestant church in Zaire. It has never been dependent on any missionary help.

3. The Pentecostal movement

Third, the outbreak of the Pentecostal movement. The rapid growth of Pentecostalism has become an important part of the story of world missions this century. More will be written on this theme in a later chapter, but it is important to make one particular point now. The contribution of Pentecostalism to world mission has been a very varied one. Without question, the enthusiasm of Pentecostals in the West for missions has been notable. The commitment of European and North American Pentecostals to missionary work at a time when the enthusiasm of other mainstream denominations was waning is significant. But perhaps even more importantly, many of the independent churches around the world owe their origins to a Pentecostal inspiration. Pentecostal experience, expectations and spirituality underpin a great deal of the growth of the church around the world, even when it is not directly acknowledged.

The very fluidity of the Pentecostal movement leads to the blurring of many boundaries. For example, one of the most important black church leaders in South Africa has been Nicholas Bhengu. During the 1970s Bhengu spent a term at the Selly Oak Colleges in Birmingham, England, where I spoke with him. Even then, Bhengu was frequently described as 'the black man's Billy Graham'. Apart from any indirect effect of his work on bringing people to Christ in large meetings, Bhengu's work led directly to the formation of over 1000 congregations. But from a strictly ecclesiastical perspective, Bhengu's work would have to be listed as part of the American Assemblies of God overseas mission work. This is a rather misleading designation. When I asked Bhengu whether the direction of his work came from the Assemblies of God or not, he laughed and said, 'I am the Assemblies of God in South Africa!' This was not a boast, it was simply a statement of reality. Bhengu was pleased to be affiliated to the Assemblies of God. For many years it solved the problem of church registration in South Africa. In addition, there were occasions when American missionaries and funds were helpful. Moreover, Bhengu genuinely delighted in multiracial contacts and conversation. But at a grass-roots level, Bhengu's work is genuinely African.

Even in the case of the Kimbanguist church the boundaries are unclear. Despite Simon Kimbangu's Baptist roots, the characteristics of his movement are clearly much more Pentecostal than they are Baptist. When the Kimbanguist church was welcomed into the World Council of Churches, a Pentecostal denomination, the Brasil para Christo, joined at the same time. Walter Hollenweger notes of this occasion: '. . . the Brazilian Pentecostal leader Manoel de Melo named the chef spirituel of the Kimbanguists, Joseph Diangienda, a Pentecostal, while the latter promoted de Melo to be a Kimbanguist.'[13]

4. Spontaneous outbreak of revival

The situation becomes even more complicated when we come to consider the fourth factor — the spontaneous outbreak of revival. Whether in East Africa, South America or South East Asia, the unexpected flow of revival fervour has caused the church to be strengthened, not only in the location of revival itself but in missionary zeal beyond the revival. As the author J. Edwin Orr has demonstrated, revivals make excellent subjects for study and for writing. One aspect of revival which is worthy of special note is the extent to which revival carries the potential to change the orientation of whole societies as well as simply to add to the numerical strength of the church. Three rather different examples serve to illustrate the point.

The dramatic growth of Christianity in North East India, in Nagaland and Mizoram, has led to a situation where some 80 to 95 per cent of the population are practising Christians. At the beginning of this century the church hardly existed in these places. The work of missionaries was clearly important and the assistance of national Christians essential, but the efforts of both foreign missionaries and nationals were far outstripped by the effect of spontaneous revival. Having been largely tribal peoples with animist religious systems, these populations have become what Roger Hedlund calls, 'one of the most "Christian" places on earth'.[14] Hedlund goes on to comment: 'Prior to a recent election, churches in Mizoram spent two entire nights in prayer. The culture has been transformed by Christian values.'[15]

The changes have indeed been dramatic. The headhunters of Nagaland have seen an end to the misery of constant tribal conflict, revenge and killing. These two states now have the highest literacy rates of any population on the Indian sub-continent. All this change has taken place within living memory.

Far reaching as the effects might be, Nagaland and Mizoram have long been cultural islands at the fringes of the dominant Hindu culture. In Indonesia, it has been possible to see revival impacting a much more complex society and, moreover, one which has been overwhelmingly Muslim. There is some dispute about the extent to which it is proper to speak about the vast population of Indonesia (close to 200 million people) as a thoroughly Islamic society. There is also some debate as to whether the majority of converts that have come through the revival are either tribal peoples on the edge of Islam, or part of the indigenous Chinese population with an older tradition drawn from the mix of Confucianism, Buddhism and Taoism that often characterises Chinese communities. However, what we can say is that at the beginning of the century the Christian church in Indonesia was tiny. The Indonesian revival which began in the 1960s and which is still fuelling significant church growth today, has resulted in the creation of a strong, vibrant and expanding Christian church where little progress had previously been seen.

It is a very sensitive matter to speak about actual figures and percentages in the Indonesian situation. Indonesian Christians are sure that the official figures significantly understate the size of the Christian community and they are not anxious to challenge these statements in public. It is neither wise nor necessary to speculate on what the real figure might be. No-one disputes that the Christian community is disproportionately well represented in government, business and other circles of influence. The Indonesian government claims that the total strength of the Christian community comprises some 9.6 per cent of the population. That percentage translates to some 17.5 million people, the majority of whom have become Christians since 1965. Almost by definition the extent of conversion growth in this land has been astonishing by any measure.

A very different scenario is presented by the situation in South America. The very varied societies in South America have traditionally been viewed as almost entirely Christian in the sense that they fell under the broad aegis of Catholicism. However a closer look at these communities reveals a much more complex local reality. Certainly the Roman Catholic church is strong and holds the allegiance of many people at every level in these societies. But in many cases Catholicism has been mixed with a degree of spiritism and animism that leaves open to question the idea that South America has ever been a totally Christian continent. Much the same has been said of Europe in the Middle Ages.

Protestant missions began work in South and Latin America in the latter part of the nineteenth century. At the beginning of the twentieth century the total Protestant community in the whole of South America was estimated to be a mere 50,000 people. Current estimates suggest that this figure will have grown to some 100 million people by the year 2000. Clearly, something more than just successful missionary work has been in operation here. It is not true to say that South America has experienced one single and continuous revival movement. It is more accurate to speak in terms of a mixture of localised revivals over a long period combined with the very active witness of indigenous Pentecostal churches. In South America, the Protestant church is overwhelmingly, though not entirely, Pentecostal.

The impact of this combination of mission, Pentecostal witness, indigenous independent churches and revival has been to raise the question about the future character of South American society. Even secular periodicals have begun to ask the question, 'Is South America becoming Protestant?'[16] The implication, seen very clearly by secular observers, is that this Protestant shift is beginning to change the culture of that continent. The Protestant work ethic may yet prove to be more powerful in South American society than the intervention of the World Bank.

5. *Cross-cultural mission*

The final factor in helping to produce numerical growth has been the development of cross-cultural mission on the part of those who live in the recently evangelised parts of our globe. The missionary activity emerging from these new sources stretches the imagination. South Korea is now one of the most active countries engaged in mission. Some twelve months before writing these words I met a Korean who is serving as a missionary in a strongly Muslim country. Within a few months of his arrival as a missionary he was witnessing actively to a significant number of people. Part of the reason for the opportunities that came to him sprang from his nationality. Few people in that land even imagined that Christians were ever anything other than white and Western. This man defied their stereotypes. My Korean acquaintance wanted to give all the credit to his prayer team. He told me that he had recruited a number of prayer partners from his home church who were committed to pray for him early each morning. I asked him how many partners he had. I suppose that I had a figure of twelve or so in my mind — a cell group. He responded by telling me that he had 2000 prayer partners. He was breaking some of my stereotypes too!

Increasingly, there are cross-cultural missionaries within

India. Christians from the stronger Christian communities in the South of India are helping to evangelise the Hindu heartlands of North India. It is much harder to dismiss Christianity as the religion of white colonialists when it arrives in national dress. It is also impossible to deny South Indians a visa!

Missionaries from Sri Lanka are helping to found churches amongst the Sri Lankan and Indian diaspora in places as diverse as California, Singapore, Paris, Copenhagen and London. The same is true for other displaced communities, whether Chinese or Indian. Missionaries from Portuguese-speaking Brazil are finding their way to the former Portuguese colonies of Angola and Mozambique as well as to Portugal itself. Spanish-speaking workers from South American lands are being mobilised for mission. There are even instances of missionaries from mainland China seeking to spread the gospel in Tibet — a land closed to the West.

These missionaries look much more like the missionaries we read about in the New Testament. Unlike so much mission from the powerful West, these missionaries are not the rich speaking to the poor, or the powerful speaking to the weak, with all the confused messages that such mission brings. Interestingly, the fact that mission sometimes comes from the poor to the rich, as it does with Filipino and Indian house-servants in the Middle East, actually overcomes the suspicion that greets the Western missionary. The well-known plea of an Indian Christian at Edinburgh 1910 — 'You have given your bodies to be burned. We also ask for love. Give us friends'[17] — is fulfilled in the cross-cultural mission exercised by the poor.

The whole wide world for Jesus

This rapid growth in the total number of Christians in our world has produced some very fundamental shifts in the nature of the world-wide Christian family. Even though the Christian faith began as a reform movement within Judaism, there is good evidence that within a few years of the founding of the Christian faith it included Christians from Africa, the near East and the Middle East as well as from Europe. During the first few centuries the natural home of Christianity was the Mediterranean basin. North Africa was a strong centre of the Christian faith. As I have already noted, by the year 1000 Christianity was overwhelmingly European in its orientation. In the year 1900, 83 per cent of the world's Christians lived in Europe or North America. English was the dominant language of the Protestant church. Today, less than ninety years after Edinburgh 1910, 60 per cent of the world's Christians live in Africa, Asia, Latin America and the Pacific.[18] As many Christians now speak Spanish as they do English.[19] We can argue that since about 1960 Christianity has, for the first time in its history, become a genuinely world-wide religion. This is undoubtedly the fruit of the modern missionary movement in this century.

This decisive shift in the world orientation of Christianity has brought with it a number of other demographic changes in the Christian family. First, there is now a non-white majority amongst Christians. Second, the numerical balance of Christianity is moving from the Northern hemisphere to the Southern hemisphere. There are 771 million Christians living in Africa, Latin America, East Asia and Oceania compared to 705 million Christians who live in North America, Europe and the former USSR. The balance of the world's Christians, 143 million, live in South Asia. Third, there is a growing trend towards the poorer countries of the world. Two out of every five Christians now live in poor countries.

This demographic shift represents a huge expansion of the church through conversion growth. Before the advent of the modern missionary movement most Christians were part of the Christian family largely because they had inherited the faith from generations of believers before them. This is no longer true. An increasing number of the world's Christians are either first-generation Christians or can point to their parents or grandparents as the first Christians in their immediate family. This contrasts sharply with Islam. Although it is perfectly true that Islam is growing faster in percentage terms than Christianity, a much higher proportion of Islam's growth stems simply from high levels of population growth in the countries of Muslim strength. More than half of all the world's Muslims live in four countries and three of these countries are in the Indian sub-continent. They are all countries with very high population growth.

The combination of these major shifts in the composition of the Christian faith has huge implications for the future of Christianity in general and for missions in particular. The dream of the Edinburgh delegates to evangelise (although not necessarily to convert) the world in a single generation has still not been completed although it has come a good deal closer than some sceptics might have imagined. The future initiative in mission may now lie outside the Western world. Even though the West still has a contribution to make in mission, as we stand at the end of the twentieth century it is impossible to imagine a world missionary conference dominated by British and American delegates. It is even more impossible to imagine such a conference without a single African delegate. The future task of mission no longer consists of an exclusively Anglo-Saxon mandate. It will never again be mission from the West to everywhere else. Mission now properly belongs to every one of the six continents in our world and will take place in all of those continents. The task of winning the West needs now to be seen in the context of this new reality.

Notes

1. Max Warren, *Social History and Christian Mission* pp. 275ff.
2. *Ibid.*, p. 30.
3. Cited in Max Warren, *op. cit.*, p. 155.
4. Stephen Neill, *A History of Christian Missions*, p. 560.

5. This debate is discussed by Walter Hollenweger in *Evangelism Today*.

6. *International Review of Mission*, 1968.

7. Joel Carpenter and Wilbert Shenk (eds.), *Earthen Vessels*, p. xii.

8. J. Bonk, *Mission and Money*, p. 73.

9. Max Warren, *op. cit.*, p. 179.

10. Roland Allen, *The Spontaneous Expansion of the Church*, p. 27.

11. Lamin Sanneh, *Toward the 21st Century*, pp. 85ff.

12. Bengt Sundkler, *Zulu Zion*, pp. 15ff.

13. Walter Hollenweger, *Pentecost between Black and White*, pp. 55ff.

14. Roger Hedlund, *Evangelization and Church Growth*, pp. 38ff.

15. *Ibid.*

16. This suggestion is commented on in *MARC Newsletter*, June 1994, p. 2. It also records some projections of the growth of the Protestant community in a list of Latin American countries.

17. Ruth Rouse and Stephen Neill (eds.), *A History of the Ecumenical Movement, Vol. 1*, p. 359.

18. Andrew Walls, St. Colm's Lecture, p. 3.

19. Bryant Myers, *The Changing Shape of World Mission*, p. 10.

CHAPTER FIVE

ONE FAITH, ONE LORD, ONE CHURCH?

The organisers of Edinburgh 1910 had taken a huge leap of imagination in seeking to include Christians from beyond the evangelical world. Their goal had been both to marshall the greatest possible level of resource for world mission and to overcome the disunity which sometimes marred the work of the gospel overseas. The twentieth century has seen the emergence of the ecumenical movement as a powerful force which has acted to influence the character and shape of the world-wide church. Church historians trace the origins of the ecumenical movement to Edinburgh 1910.

However, it is highly questonable as to whether the unity pursued so assiduously by those in the ecumenical tradition is quite the same as that envisaged by the evangelical organisers of Edinburgh. The twentieth century has seen both the pursuit of Christian unity on the one hand and the development of an unprecedented new division of Christianity on the other hand. This new division has used the words 'liberal' or even 'ecumenical' or 'conciliar' to describe one party and the term 'evangelical' or 'fundamentalist' to describe the other party. Few are entirely comfortable with the use of these terms. They are often called 'labels'. Part of the unease lies in the fact that all of these terms have been used as terms of abuse as much as to describe a particular tradition in any objective sense.

The crude characterisation of each party is that ecumenicals are interested in Christian unity but not in evangelism while evangelicals are interested in evangelism but not in Christian unity. These are the stones thrown by each side across what has become a deep divide. They are also accusations which each side strongly refutes. Ecumenicals want to claim that they are just as interested in evangelism and mission as anyone else but they see Christian unity as an important prerequisite for effective outreach. Evangelicals want to insist that they are also anxious to see Christians working with each other but not if that means compromising the truth of the gospel.

How then can it be that a movement which traces its roots to a conference organised by evangelicals and which stands in a long tradition of evangelical action, should develop in such a way that many evangelicals were not only increasingly absent from it but positively hostile to its intentions? The breadth and strength of unity experienced at Edinburgh, with everyone from Anglo-Catholics to revivalist evangelicals present, was shattered by developments which had been gathering pace quietly in the last half of the nineteenth century. These controversies were to impact the Christian world as a debate between modernists and traditionalists. The issue in question was that of biblical interpretation.

Pressures had been building for many years as the work of German theologians in the field of biblical criticism gradually made themselves felt in the Anglo-Saxon world. It only needed a catalyst to produce profound unease, and that event arrived with the publication of Darwin's theories on evolution. Controversy has a way of producing camps when none need develop and this is exactly what took place. At a very basic level the process at work was that of the adjustment of Christianity to modernity. Interestingly, both sides in the dispute had no doubt at all of the value of science and indeed sought to use arguments from both science and theology to support their perspective.

The one side, those who identified themselves with a liberal position, took the view that Christian revelation needed to be seen in the light of modern discoveries while the more conservative position wanted to defend the faith against the onslaught of the modern world. As the historian Mark Noll comments, '. . . each felt that the other was damaging the defence of the faith in the modern world.'[1]

To a very considerable extent, it was the liberal position that won the day. Noll, almost certainly correctly, takes the view that the liberal position, '. . . won its most important victories in centers of higher learning rather than in the churches, where a moderate conservatism tended to prevail throughout the early twentieth century'.[2] Although Noll is describing the situation in North America, much the same could be said of the European scene.

These victories won in the places of 'higher learning' were crucial in that they allowed the leadership of the denominations to be increasingly won to a liberal position. The clergy of the major denominations were trained in schools imbued with an acceptance of Biblical Criticism, or Higher Criticism as it is sometimes called. It was these leaders who predominated increasingly in the emerging ecumenical tradition. The more conservative position tended to loose its voice and indeed its confidence. As the major historic Protestant denominations became increasingly identified both with ecumenism and with a liberal theological perspective, it was inevitable that over time the two terms became almost interchangeable. From the perspective of the losing party, to be liberal was to be ecumenical, to be ecumenical was to be liberal and so against a conservative or evangelical position. Evangelicals therefore felt alienated from the very movement that they had helped to birth!

A movement matures

The ecumenical leader Visser 't Hooft identifies three major phases in the development of the ecumenical movement.[3]

The first is what he calls the period of the pioneers. He identifies the organisers of the Edinburgh conference, Mott and Oldham, as two of those pioneers. The promoters of the Faith and Order Movement, Brent and Gardiner, and the founder of the Life and Work Movement, Archbishop Soderblom, were other key figures. Many of the leading figures associated with these initiatives were clearly from an evangelical background. Their work brought into being many of the basic frameworks around which it was possible to build a broader world movement aimed at producing a climate of Christian co-operation and unity.

The Faith and Order Movement held two key conferences, one in Lausanne in 1927 and the second in Edinburgh in 1937. The Life and Work stream also held a number of formative conferences. The first was called a preparatory conference and took place in Geneva in 1920. The second was held in Stockholm in 1925 and a third was organised in Oxford in 1937. Both the Faith and Order conferences and the Life and Work events were strongly parallel movements. Their conferences helped and informed each other. Both streams were rightly called movements and many critical developments took place between the major conferences, some at national as well as at an international level.

The International Missionary Council, which was brought into being in 1921 at a meeting in the State of New York, held what it called Council meetings in Jerusalem in 1928, Tambaram near Madras in 1938 and Whitby, Ontario in 1947. Although the term 'Council' was used, these meetings were much closer in their format to the conferences that the Faith and Order and Life and Work Movements were holding.

The second phase involved giving more specific shape to these early moves. Visser't Hooft suggests that this phase had three tasks: to try and integrate the various ecumenical streams, to relate these bodies much more directly to the life of the various Christian denominations and to attempt to devise a specific programme of common action. The year

1937 was particularly important in this process. Both the Faith and Order and the Life and Work Movements held major conferences in Britain during that year. It was proposed that both these bodies should be brought together in a single organisation and that the joint body would maintain a close relationship with the International Missionary Council. Within a year a constitution was formulated that was to act as the basis for the creation of the World Council of Churches. The advent of the Second World War inevitably delayed the process. The first Assembly was to have been held in 1941 but in the event it was not possible for the first Assembly of the World Council of Churches to meet until 1948.

The inauguration of the World Council of Churches, meeting in Amsterdam in 1948, marks the beginning of what Visser't Hooft calls the third period. By this time, most of the pioneers were no longer active in church life. A new generation of leaders began to build the organisational phase of the ecumenical movement. In common with the earlier phases of the movement, the World Council of Churches has been based to some extent around the pivotal Assemblies held in Evanston, Illinois in 1954, New Delhi in 1961, Uppsala in 1968, Nairobi in 1975, Vancouver in 1983 and Canberra in 1991. The International Missionary Council was merged with the World Council at the 1961 Assembly. This act finally brought together all of the various streams, most of which had looked back to Edinburgh 1910 as their inspiration.

By the time of the 1954 Evanston Assembly the opposition of evangelicals, particularly in North America, to the ecumenical movement was implacable. Although a few who would call themselves evangelicals were present at all of the World Council's Assemblies and remained in active communication with the International Missionary Council, they were very lonely voices. Evangelical opposition was strengthened by an increasing perception on the part of many conservative evangelicals that the World Council was more interested in political involvement than in preaching the gospel. No single programme of the World Council did more to reinforce this feeling than the Programme to Combat Racism. The various grants made by this programme to liberation movements, especially in Southern Africa, placed considerable strain on relationships within the Council and gave much ammunition to its opponents.

In more recent years, the isolation of evangelicals from the affairs of the World Council has moderated. Three factors have helped in this process. First, some of the younger churches which have been members of the Council for many years have tended to become increasingly evangelical in their leadership as national leadership has emerged to replace that of their sponsoring missionary bodies. Second, a number of Pentecostal and Independent churches which have maintained a strong evangelical witness, such as the Kimbanguists already mentioned, have joined the Council and strengthened the witness of the younger churches.

Third, evangelicals from some of the historic churches in the West, notably Anglican evangelicals, have made a determined effort to become involved in the affairs of the Council. The Nairobi Assembly in 1975 was notable for the strength of the evangelical voice and witness in its midst. While it would be foolish to say that the World Council of Churches has overcome the suspicions of the evangelical world, nevertheless the evangelical contribution to the affairs of the Council may well become felt increasingly in the century to come.

A wider ecumenism

It would be wrong to suggest that the World Council of Churches and the ecumenical movement are entirely synonymous. While it is true that the World Council seeks to serve the ecumenical movement and has an important role within that movement, the broader movement towards Christian unity is a far wider matter than this one institution.

Although it is true that the official Vatican response to the ecumenical movement was very distant before the Second Vatican Council, responses since that time have been markedly different. Although not members of the World Council, the Catholic church now sends observers to the World Council of Churches Assemblies and is active in many local and national Councils of Churches in various parts of the world. The Vatican has instituted many ecumenical initiatives which centre on a series of dialogues with major confessional bodies. Dialogues with church families as diverse as the Orthodox church, the Lutherans, the Methodists, the Disciples of Christ, the Pentecostals and even the Charismatic movement have become a commonplace occurrence in Vatican thinking.

In addition to these interconfessional initiatives, the earlier nineteenth-century trend towards the creation of world-wide confessional organisations has continued throughout the twentieth century. Pentecostals and a host of smaller denominational families have all attempted to build connections within their church families.

Ironically, despite their common opposition to the World Council of Churches, evangelicals have been active in organising national and international events which mirror to some extent the activities of the ecumenical movement. In their own way evangelicals have continued their separate quest for a greater degree of unity and co-operation amongst Christians.

At national and at local level the degree of unity amongst Christians makes the hostile positions adopted by Christians towards those of other denominations in past years seem almost unbelievable. The historian Adrian Hastings captures the feeling of denominational hostility that prevailed at the end of the nineteenth century and the beginning of the twentieth century. He cites an occasion in 1899 when the highly respected Baptist minister, F. B. Meyer, wrote to the Anglican High Churchman, the Bishop of Southwark,

Edward Talbot. He asked if he might be willing to visit their centenary Sunday School celebration when 4000 Sunday School children from Southwark would be present. Meyer wrote:

> Would it be quite impossible for you to look in? We are some of your other sheep . . . it would be a noble act of Catholicity . . . Is not the time come when such an act would be understood and appreciated by thousands outside the churches as an expression of true Christianity?[4]

It seems that it was 'quite impossible' for Bishop Talbot to accept such an invitation. Hastings points out that it was a 'matter of clear principle' that he should not do so. Although at the end of the twentieth century it might still be possible to find isolated sects who might still take such a stance, it would seem impossible for any public figure in any of the major denominations to take such a position. The warm thaw that has taken place amongst ordinary Christians in the pews of most churches has rendered insular denominationalism a thing of the past. We should not underestimate the extent of this achievement in the arena of informal ecumenism.

Ecumenical limitations

However, despite the welcome move toward an ever-increasing degree of co-operation between Christians across previously uncrossable boundaries, the limits of ecumenical strivings have also become apparent. The formal intention of the twentieth-century ecumenical movement has not been just to encourage Christians to recognise one another and to work with each other in practical projects. It has been the frequently expressed goal of the ecumenical movement to bring into being unity at an organic institutional level. The ecclesiastical reality is that there are considerably more denominations in existence at the end of the twentieth century than there were at the beginning. According to one estimate there are 23,500 denominations in the world and more are coming into being all the time.[5] There are said to be more than 400 black-led, largely Pentecostal denominations in Britain alone. None of these bodies existed fifty years ago.

The actual record of attempts to produce united churches has not been very encouraging. A listing of union schemes attempted between 1910 and 1952 appears in *A History of the Ecumenical Movement 1517–1948*. Although there have been successful union schemes since 1952, the overall pattern demonstrated by this listing remains largely unchanged. It demonstrates that the overwhelming balance of union schemes have taken place between denominations within the same ecclesiastical family, for example, unions of various Methodist, Baptist or Lutheran churches in particular nations. In many cases the unions have been between denominations that were formed separately because of patterns of immigration or through mission work undertaken by the same confessional groups operating from different countries. For example, in the United States, Lutherans who began as separate Norwegian, Swedish and German churches have in some cases been able to unite as ethnic origins became less important. In Brazil, churches formed by different Lutheran missionary societies were able to unite.

In addition to unions within ecclesiastical families, there have been successful attempts to produce united churches across more pronounced denominational barriers. In countries as diverse as Burma, Canada, Puerto Rico and India some significant united churches have come into being. However, the record demonstrates that following union, it has often (and some would argue always) been the case that instead of union producing growth in evangelism and mission, the result has often been retrenchment and decline. Even in those cases where schemes of union have resulted in continued growth, such growth has often been far slower than that experienced by those denominations that did not unite. Moreover, the same situations have also seen the formation of many new denominations in the very places where union schemes were intended to produce a united witness.

Much the same process has been observed even when the scheme of union has been a purely local matter. Some have commented, rather cynically, that in Britain the quickest way to help a local Methodist church to decline is to encourage it to unite with a local United Reformed Church. Such comment is often unfair and fails to take account of the difficulties of many of these local situations or indeed to reflect what might have taken place if no union had occurred at all. Yet nevertheless, it does point to an acute dilemma that has often faced the proponents of an ecumenism devoted entirely to a goal of organic union.

Ecumenism without mission

Those who have worked tirelessly for the goal of organic Christian unity would want to claim that the motive remains that of presenting a more effective mission to the world. Perhaps the most quoted scripture in ecumenical circles is that of the prayer of Jesus in John 17:21, 'May they be one, so that the world may believe that you sent me' (Good News Bible). Why then does there often seem to be a disjunction between ecumenical endeavour and subsequent church growth? Those from an evangelical persuasion might want to argue that the real problem lies not so much in the adoption of an attempt to produce Christian unity as in a linkage between that goal and a very liberal theological approach. Such an argument is extremely contentious and evidence can be cited both for and against such a case. However, there does seem to be a difference between the earlier evangelical passion for mission which saw attemps to unite Christians as only one aspect of that concern, and a passion for unity which can all too easily conclude that

Christian unity by itself produces a more effective missionary unit. While there may be conditions in which a united witness does produce more effective mission there is not an inevitable correlation between these two concerns.

The development of the ecumenical movement reveals that expectations of the outcome of ecumenism depend to a considerable extent on the questions that ecumenism is designed to solve. The historical perspectives of the participants inevitably affect those expectations. There are at least five very different potential perspectives which have been brought to the ecumenical table.

1. Ecumenism as a programme of social reform

The evangelical movement on both sides of the Atlantic had maintained a strong emphasis on social reform throughout the nineteenth century. In Britain, that programme is most clearly seen in the complex initiatives of those such as Lord Shaftesbury and others in the Clapham Sect to bring a Christian influence to bear on society. That same concern is reflected in early ecumenical initiatives in the United States. The formation of the Federal Council of Churches of Christ in 1908 in the United States consisted of thirty three Protestant denominations with an astonishing 18,000,000 members. As Mark Noll suggests, the theological basis was very limited — 'to manifest the essential oneness of the Christian churches of America in Jesus Christ as their divine Lord and Savior'. But their practical concern is much more evident — 'to secure a larger combined influence for the churches of Christ in all matters affecting the moral and social condition of the people, so as to promote the application of the law of Christ in every relation of human life.'[6]

The serious division amongst Christians in the United States following the modernist–fundamentalism controversies severely weakened this Protestant attempt to influence, lead and shape the public life of the nation. Thereafter, the expectations brought to ecumenical endeavour began to change.

2. Ecumenism as healing a fractious Christendom

The much older wounds of Europe, dating back to the Reformation and the subsequent religious wars, had a profound impact on the soul of European civilization. The theologian Wolfhart Pannenberg points to these conflicts as constituting one of the profound influences in the secularization of Europe. For many churchmen in Europe, the division of Christians was a 'scandal'. The use of this word carries the memory of the bitter wounds coming from the time when Christians would literally wound and indeed kill each other on the battlefield. By the time of the nineteenth and early twentieth centuries the division of Christianity was solely a war of words and sentiment. But there still remained a sense that Europe was the inheritor of Christendom and that Christendom remained divided. The advent of the First World War came as a bitter reminder of earlier conflicts. Although this twentieth-century conflict had more to do with the competition of nationhood and empire and far less to do with creeds and doctrine, there was still a strident claim by every side that God and the church vindicated their cause.

The post-Edinburgh desire for Christian unity was also inevitably a post-First World War desire for unity. That made a difference. It was not now so much a concern for Christians to work together for overseas missions (although that did not disappear) as a passionate desire to ensure that Christendom could be reunited in such a way that the Christian nations of Europe would never again be in conflict. In this sense, the quest for Christian unity has its parallel in the secular world with the League of Nations and, later in the twentieth century, in the creation of the European Community. Both organisations depend to some extent on a view of Western civilisation that flows to us from an older Christendom.

Although the situation in the United States is much more complex than just this one consideration, it is still noticeable that the denominations which have remained ecumenically committed in that land are those which have a stronger sense of their European origin as compared with those which have a strong identity with American history alone. In this reading of the ecumenical movement, Christendom does not consist of Europe alone but of those lands which share in a broader Western culture. The ecumenical movement is therefore needed to heal the wounds of Christendom both in their home and exported forms.

3. The ecumenical movement as the end of isolation

One of the significant achievements of the ecumenical movement has been to re-establish contact with the many Eastern and Oriental Orthodox churches. But the perspective of the Orthodox churches in approaching the ecumenical movement could hardly be more different from that of the nineteenth-century evangelical pioneers. The Orthodox churches certainly saw ecumenical councils as a way of restoring unity to the church. Indeed it had long been their contention that the unity of the church had been ruptured precisely because the church in the West had held Councils which the Eastern churches did not recognise as belonging to the whole church. From an Orthodox perspective, changes in practice and doctrine had entered the church through these illegitimate Councils. The prospect of an ecumenical movement which emphasised broadly based Councils of the whole church appealed to the Orthodox mind.

Participation in the ecumenical movement has helped to overcome the isolation of the Orthodox community. That isolation had been imposed by a combination of factors; the increased division with a West in which the old Empire of Rome had collapsed and which had subsequently taken a rather different theological direction from that of the Eastern churches, and the growing strength of Islam in the territories which had been the ancient centres of the Eastern church. The isolation had been reinforced by divisions within Orthodoxy and in more recent times by the pressure of Communist governments in many areas of Orthodox strength. Although it is true that the Orthodox church has begun to engage in mission in more recent times, mission was not a major consideration in the interest of the Orthodox churches in the ecumenical movement.

4. Ecumenism as a Protestant phenomenon

Even though some at Edinburgh 1910 expressed the strong desire to see Roman Catholic and Orthodox representation in such meetings, only the Orthodox churches have become full partners in the ecumenical process. The Roman Catholic church took the early view that this was a Protestant phenomenon which needed to be carefully studied and considered, but the advent of the Second Vatican Council (interestingly called an ecumenical Council) in the 1960s signalled the beginning of a much more complex relationship with the ecumenical movement.

Vatican II began a process which has led to the ending of the Roman Catholic church as entirely uniform in every respect. Nowhere has this been more felt than in the liturgy itself. The Roman Catholic church now relates positively to the ecumenical movement without actually being a member of the World Council of Churches. Just as significantly, the Roman Catholic church is also being changed from within by that same movement. But change is not just coming from that source. Perhaps more than any other single communion, the Roman Catholic church has undergone a significant shift in the geographical distribution of its membership. Some observers suggest that the next Bishop of Rome will come not from Italy, Poland or Europe at all but from Africa or Latin America. The growth through mission of the Catholic community is part of the process of change encouraged or permitted by Vatican II.

The direct consequence of this complex process is that the Catholic approach to the ecumenical movement can vary enormously depending on what part of the world one is speaking from. In Britain, the Catholic contribution is considerable and does not differ a great deal from an agenda that sees the healing of the wounds of Christendom as important. But such an agenda might differ greatly in other parts of the world.

5. Ecumenism as a quest for human solidarity

Who is included in the whole house? The development of the ecumenical movement has become strongly identified since the post-war period with a more liberal theological approach. In part, that theological approach has been strengthened by the voices of the younger churches from the mission fields. It is an open question as to whether the voices from the younger churches are genuinely indigenous contributions of emerging Asian, Latin American or African theologies or whether they are the voices of a few from those lands who have been thoroughly imbued with a Western liberal theological tradition and who are only contextualising that tradition. However one chooses to answer that question, it is undeniable that the ecumenical movement in the second half of the twentieth century has become very interested in issues of human concern such as power, racism, justice, political structures, liberation and economics. That perspective has a radical impact on the perspective that is brought to the question of mission.

A crisis for mission

The missions historian and theologian, David Bosch, has written of the 'crisis of missions'.[7] The crisis to which he refers is really a crisis of confidence. He points to a number of factors that have contributed to this sense of crisis. A good number of the factors outlined by Bosch relate strongly to the central shift outlined earlier in this book, namely the emergence of the West as a major mission field in its own right. In the context of the West, Christianity has been strongly attacked by a growing secularisation, by the emergence of other ideologies such as communism, by the renewal of other world faiths and by a growing sense of guilt as the connection between mission and colonialism and imperialism has become clear. The uncertainty as to where the mission field really lies had raised the question as to what mission really is.

But what Bosch does not address is the extent to which the crisis in mission is really part of a broader crisis in Western theological thinking. Long before the acknowledged crisis in missions thinking, the actual commitment of the historic mainstream churches in the West to missions was beginning to lessen. It does not matter whether you measure that commitment in missions giving or in the recruitment of personnel, the traditional sources of missionary endeavour amongst Protestant churches in the West have declined substantially as the twentieth century has progressed.

The decline in missions commitment mirrors a loss of confidence not just in missionary activity but in the gospel message itself. The decline of the mainstream Protestant churches in the West stands in acute contrast with the growth of the evangelical movement in the West. Moreover, we cannot speak about a crisis of missions amongst evangelicals but rather about the growth of a commitment to missions in the same period.

This contrast is reflected in the very different agenda for mission exhibited by churches which stand mainly in the ecumenical tradition of the twentieth century and those who have stood either at the periphery of that movement or who have actively opposed it. The World Council of Churches has spoken of an agenda for missions which consists of the following elements:

1. Justice and peace
2. Dialogue with other religions
3. A concern for creation

By contrast, the agenda for mission exhibited by evangelicals has centred almost entirely on the central question of the practical proclamation of the gospel message. This proclamation is understood as communicating the message of the gospel in such a way that individuals and people groups encounter the risen Christ so that they will call him Lord and seek to become his disciples. It means establishing the church in every culture as the most important means by which societies may be influenced and changed.

Until relatively recently, evangelicals could rightly have been accused of seeing mission and evangelism as almost synonymous terms. To evangelise was to be engaged in mission. To be engaged in mission was to evangelise. In such a climate, in contrast with their nineteenth-century forebears, evangelicals almost became hostile to the idea of social action in any form. The polemical stance of some evangelicals was to see their own community as engaged in evangelism and their liberal opponents as interested only in social action, sometimes called pejoratively the 'social gospel'.

More recent times have seen evangelicals moderating their stand considerably and recovering their earlier commitment to social action. But the social concern of evangelicals has been self-consciously connected to their perception of social action as part of the evangelistic task.

The inclusion of a social dimension in the programme of evangelicals, together with a growing reconsideration of the place of evangelism in the life of more ecumenically committed Christians has allowed a degree of dialogue to take place between evangelicals and other Christians. That dialogue is not so much a formal discussion as the beginnings of a reassessment, by evangelicals and those Christians from other traditions, of the relationship between evangelism and mission.

The forces of evangelicalism, so divided in the earlier part of the twentieth century have become increasingly united.

The style of their growing desire for united action and witness have become strikingly similar to the impetus that gave rise to the Edinburgh Conference of 1910. At the same time, the ecumenical movement which began with that united evangelical concern and which became so detached from the evangelical movement and even detached from the priority of unity in the cause of mission, has begun to reconsider its own future. The context for this growing reassessment is both the crisis of mission within the ecumenical movement and the dramatic, unexpected growth and renewal of the evangelical movement on the stage of world Christianity. It is to the changes within the evangelical wing of the church during the twentieth century that we must now turn our attention.

Notes

1. Mark Noll, *A History of Christianity in the United States and Canada*, p. 373.
2. *Ibid.*, p. 374.
3. Visser 't Hooft, *Memoirs*, p. 3.
4. Adrian Hastings, *A History of English Christianity*, p. 86.
5. Bryant Myers, *The Changing Shape of World Mission*, p. 11.
6. Mark Noll, *op. cit.*, p. 308.
7. David Bosch, *Transforming Mission*, pp. 2ff.

CHAPTER SIX

THE EVANGELICAL RENAISSANCE

In the late nineteenth century Bishop Lightfoot, then Bishop of Durham, was an acknowledged scholar, a well-regarded churchman and a committed evangelical. His work in the North East of England enabled the Church of England to make a significant witness in those mining and industrial areas which had been influenced so powerfully by the rise of Methodism. Foremost amongst his missionary methods was his use of a group of highly committed curates, known as 'Lightfoot's lambs'. They were supposed to tackle any challenge offered to them by the Bishop, and they usually did.

The atmosphere evoked by Lightfoot's lambs was not uncommon in the powerful evangelical wing of the church throughout Britain in the late nineteenth and early twentieth century; a church that was aware that much needed to be done and was confident enough to tackle the task; a view of theology and churchmanship that was vibrant and yet generally charitable to others; conscious that there were differences of views, even within evangelicalism, and yet not bitterly divided; wanting to bring the light of the gospel to bear on the problems of society while remaining thoroughly involved in the culture of the time. Many of those who were Lightfoot's lambs were of that variety of muscular Christianity that was also espoused by world leaders such as Theodore Roosevelt. These were attractive individuals able to cut a dash in whatever sphere of activity they found themselves. Many of those who were part of evangelical Christianity were admired in society more widely. In Britain the leading cricketers C. T. Studd and W. G. Grace were known for their strong evangelical Christian commitment. Studd actually gave up cricket for a career as an overseas missionary.

That was the position on both sides of the Atlantic prior to 1910. Yet little more than a decade later the cause of evangelical Christianity had become so weakened that it had almost faded into obscurity. What could have caused such a cataclysmic change?

The fundamentalist furore

The growing debate between Christianity and a newly emergent secularism had developed in unsurprising ways during the latter part of the nineteenth century. Darwin's theories on evolution formed an important plank in the general Scientism of secularist apologists such as T. H. Huxley.[1] There was no general agreement amongst evangelical Christians concerning a response to these attacks. In keeping with its older tradition, evangelicals were interested in maintaining an enquiring and lively involvement with new intellectual developments and in seeking to relate a Christian vision to them. There was certainly no significant difference between the response of evangelicals and those of other varieties of churchmanship to issues such as evolutionary theory. However, a gradual change did begin to emerge as a group of thinkers who we might call somewhat loosely 'modernists' began to gain significant influence in the universities and colleges, particularly in the United States. This development was particularly notable amongst Presbyterians, if only because of their significant commitment to education and their rigorous intellectual tradition. Difficult intellectual challenges were not likely to be ignored by those in such a tradition.

A useful signpost of the pressures that were beginning to mount came with the publication in the United States of a series of booklets called *The Fundamentals: A Testimony to the Truth*. Nearly a hundred different booklets were published between 1910 and 1915. They were written by leading evangelicals from both sides of the Atlantic and were intended to defend or outline the basic truths which Christians upheld. The context for these articles was clearly the sense that some core doctrines, if not all, were under attack and needed to be reaffirmed. Not the least of the fundamentals was the assertion that the Bible is the inspired word of God.

The publication of these booklets was not intended to begin a movement so much as to provoke debate. Indeed, as many have since pointed out, many of the positions taken in *The Fundamentals* were not typical of the views that later fundamentalists espoused. In particular, some of the booklets displayed an openness to the theory of evolution.[2] But the social background to the distribution of these works was that of the outbreak of war. Even though the war was a long way from America and even though the formal involvement of the United States did not take place until 1917, the nature and character of the First World War spoke to many of a wider impending social crisis. Civilisation seemed to be on the brink of annihilation. The calling into question of traditional beliefs and values seemed to be part of that cataclysm.

The title of the booklet series gave rise to a new name for a new movement. Mark Noll suggests that the term 'fundamentalist' was first used in 1920 by the Baptist editor Curtis Lee Laws, in his call to arms against those in the church who challenged traditional Christian belief. The debate became much more heated as a direct consequence of an exchange of polemical pamphlets. The first was issued in 1922 by a young preacher, Harry Emerson Fosdick, a Baptist minister who was as well known in his day as Moody and Billy Graham were in other periods. It was aimed directly at the emerging

fundamentalist movement and was entitled *Shall the Fundamentalists Win?* Originally delivered in sermon form,
130,000 copies were circulated to Protestant clergy in an
attempt to influence opinion in what was almost a marketing
exercise. The money for this rather unusual initiative came
from John D. Rockefeller.

This opening salvo was replied to with a pamphlet entitled
Shall Unbelief Win? written by Clarence Edward Macartney.
From this point on a process of polarisation and bitter fight-
ing took place. The heart of the fundamentalist position was
that of opposition — opposition to change, opposition to the
growing liberalism or modernism that was becoming such a
feature of the major Protestant denominations and opposition
to the social gospel which seemed to preach that the kingdom
of God could be established here on earth by the good works
of men. Those who took such a stance had been strongly
influenced by the dispensational premillenial position so
ardently advocated by those such as John Nelson Darby of
the Plymouth Brethren a few decades earlier. They saw in
such a theological position a way of resisting the claims of
modernisers. For some time afterwards, dispensationalism
and a premillenial position seemed to be inseparable from
the fundamentalist cause.

The stance advocated by the fundamentalists was that of
withdrawal. Their leaders had become convinced that it was
no longer possible to reform from within. New institutions
and even new denominations would need to be created in
order to save the truth of the gospel from distortion. This
process was given a significant lead by the withdrawal of
four leading scholars from Princeton Theological Seminary
to found Westminster Theological Seminary. Some of the
important early heroes of the fundamentalist position had
been former teachers at Princeton, men such as B. B. War-
field and Charles Hodge. They had not advocated withdrawal. But the men who would now lead fundamentalists did
not believe it possible to do anything other than withdraw.

This response was not informed by a particular strategy. To a very large degree it flowed from the culture-rejecting character of the fundamentalist position itself.

Not all evangelicals saw the need to withdraw. Some remained to debate, reform and influence. But the position of fundamentalism within the evangelical camp led to a division and inevitable weakening of evangelicalism as a movement. The fundamentalist controversy meant that evangelicals were involved in as much argument and hostility amongst themselves as they were with their liberal opponents.

A turning point for the fundamentalist position arrived with the well-known 'Scopes Monkey Trial' which took place in the State of Tennessee in 1925. The trial involved the prosecution of a teacher, John T. Scopes, who was accused of teaching the theory of evolution in violation of a state statute that forbade it to be taught in Tennessee public (i.e. state) schools. This local matter assumed a nation-wide importance as a *cause célèbre* for those who wished to see a strongly secular position adopted in American schools. The prosecution was led by a fundamentalist populist, William Jennings Bryan, while Scopes was defended by the much more able Clarence Darrow. The American Civil Liberties Union supported Scopes and the trial attracted nation-wide coverage.

Although Scopes was found guilty and was fined, the wider battle for the sympathies of the American public was undoubtedly won by Darrow. As Alister McGrath comments:

> . . . Bryan was declared to be unthinking, uneducated and reactionary. Fundamentalism might make sense in a rural Tennessee backwater, but had no place in sophisticated urban America. In particular, the journalist and literary critic H. L. Mencken (to whom Sinclair Lewis later dedicated *Elmer Gantry*) successfully portrayed fundamentalists as intolerant, backward and ignorant dolts who stood outside the mainstream of American culture.[3]

The position adopted by fundamentalism not only fatally divided the Protestant community, it also dealt a hammer blow to the vibrancy of evangelical witness. Its tendency to appear suspicious of broader cultural values together with its policy of separation stood in stark contrast to the earlier nineteenth-century tradition of evangelicalism. That earlier tradition had sought to be vitally involved in society, offering a vision of a reforming, relevant, and orthodox Christian faith.

The bitterness of the fundamentalist controversies did not take place in other Anglo-Saxon lands to anything like the same extent that they had in America but the confidence of evangelical witness was nevertheless influenced by the American debate. From the 1920s onwards it became increasingly difficult for evangelical Christians in Britain to distance themselves from the accusations that they were closet fundamentalists too. In both America and Britain Protestants seemed to be forced away from the centre ground. Those who were inclined to take a more liberal stance in theology were reinforced in their position by the feeling that the only real alternative was that of fundamentalism. Those who were worried by the content of a liberal theology were increasingly identified with a somewhat anti-intellectual position. The middle ground in theology had been largely lost to both sides. Evangelical Christianity seemed to be the greater loser in this divide.

Evangelical recovery

The growth of evangelical Christianity in the latter half of the twentieth century has been as dramatic as it has been unexpected. Having been discredited, largely as a consequence of the fundamentalist controversies in the United States and because of a certain loss of nerve and even narrowness elsewhere, few could have predicted the important place that evangelical Christianity would occupy in the world Christian family in the closing decades of the twentieth century. During the interwar years of defeat for evangelicals, when it seemed as if this vital movement had passed into history as an obscurantist relic of an earlier age, vital foundations were being laid. These attempts at rebuilding varied enormously from country to country but some common themes emerge.

In the United States, the possibly questionable tactic of withdrawal from the existing denominations and Protestant institutions of learning and mission had produced considerable grass-roots activity. Fundamentalism learned how to utilise an older revivalist tradition. Even though secular playwrights might parody the activities of revivalism in films such as *Elmer Gantry*, old-style revivalism had not altogether lost its appeal to some sections of the population. The depression of the 1930s led many to look for hope beyond this world as well as in it. Millions of Americans were marginalised by economic failure, and a marginalised religion was able to dig deep into these experiences of despair. In particular, old-style revivalism found new expression through the medium of radio. During the 1930s one practitioner of evangelism on the airwaves, Charles Fuller, developed an audience of some ten million people who listened to his *Old-Fashioned Revival Hour*. Many of the more conservative denominations such as the Southern Baptists, as well as many newer denominations, experienced considerable growth during this period. Such growth stood in marked contrast to the difficulties being experienced by the more liberal mainline denominations in this same period. The evangelicals were growing through the simple use of evangelism.

This revivalist stream was somewhat aided during the 1930s by the development of a new religious force in its midst. The Pentecostal denominations, both black and white, offered a new and direct religious encounter primarily amongst poorer people at this time of social dislocation.

More will be said about this new religious phenomenon in the following chapter.

Although revivalism was not such a potent force in countries such as Great Britain, nevertheless evangelical groups, particularly those associated with the Fellowship of Evangelical Churches, were beginning to organise themselves at a grass-roots level. The Pentecostal campaigns of the two Jeffreys brothers, particularly those of George Jeffreys, exercised a growing, if still minority, influence in British religious life. Some of George Jeffreys' campaigns, notably one held in the Bingley Halls in Birmingham, attracted tens of thousands of people.

However, this grass-roots movement would probably not have had much long-term significance had it not also been accompanied by some important organisational developments which laid the foundations for a much more significant growth following the Second World War.

In the United States, moves began to create an organisation which would unite a broader stream of evangelicals than that which had been identified solely with the fundamentalist camp, and the National Association of Evangelicals was formed in 1942. This grouping was sufficiently broad to include a significant number of Pentecostals, who, together with some other evangelicals, had not been included in the earlier associations. These same forces continued to create many other new organisations which enabled evangelicals to develop overseas missionary work, publishing, evangelistic agencies and youth work, and which helped to shape a new constituency in the post-war years. Equivalent agencies were also formed in other countries, although these were developed somewhat later than in the United States.

These organisational moves were paralleled by a new desire to give an intellectual underpinning to the growing strength of the evangelical cause. A significant number of evangelical scholars on both sides of the Atlantic began to be recognised as notable contributors in their area of expertise.

Particularly in biblical studies, men such as F. F. Bruce, Donald Guthrie and Donald Wiseman in Britain enabled evangelicals to enter the debate on biblical scholarship. In the United States the formation of institutions such as Fuller Theological Seminary not only worked for the very best in scholarship but maintained an openness of spirit that allowed evangelicals to reach out beyond the narrow confines of an earlier fundamentalism.

The immediate post-war years in the United States saw the outbreak of a number of revival movements which, although not on the scale of the nineteenth-century revival movements, made an impact which enabled the rather crude campaign revivalism of the 1930s to reach beyond a poor, and often entirely rural, audience to touch larger populations. Into this new milieu stepped a new style of revival preacher, more sophisticated, more aware of social issues, better organised and better financed. The earlier tent crusades were now moving into large indoor arenas. Some of those who had been itinerant evangelists began to build large church centres.

By far the best known of this new generation of preachers was the Baptist minister, Billy Graham. Immediately following the Second World War, Graham was employed by the Youth for Christ organisation. In 1949 Graham, together with others in Youth for Christ, planned a three-week crusade in Los Angeles. In the final week of the campaign reports circulated about the conversion of an unlikely combination of athletes, mobsters and entertainers. This newsworthy development led William Randolph Hearst to instruct his newspapers to promote this young evangelist. Thereafter the meetings were even better attended and were extended for a further nine weeks. This single event enabled Graham to be seen as a rising star in the evangelical firmament.

There was no equivalent revival phenomenon in an exhausted Britain immediately following the Second World War. Even the large campaigns of George Jeffreys were somewhat diminished after the war. However, a number of important developments were taking place amongst Anglican evangelicals. During the 1930s it might have been tempting for many to think that the evangelical cause was all but extinguished amongst the historic denominations, but for those able to see, it was possible to discern some foundational developments that would lead to growth in the immediate post-war period. One such contribution was the work of E. J. H. Nash, who ran evangelical camps for public school boys. Many of the next generation of Anglican evangelical leaders emerged from these camps.

One of those leaders was John Stott, who became a curate at the fashionable All Souls Church, Langham Place in London in 1945, and then its rector in 1950. For the next thirty years, All Souls was to be the cathedral of Anglican evangelicalism. Several key developments, all of which involved John Stott, occurred during the mid-1950s. Not the least of these was the decision of Anglican evangelicals to be involved in the visit of Billy Graham to conduct his first crusade at Harringay in 1954.

The decision hardly seems out of the ordinary today, but at that time there was a significant cultural boundary to be crossed. Billy Graham was a Baptist revivalist preacher brought up in the rural setting of North Carolina in a strongly fundamentalist tradition. Many of the Anglicans who wanted to associate with Graham were from metropolitan London, had public-school educations, and retained contacts with a very privileged group in society. The party of Americans travelling with Graham might have wondered what they had become involved in when they met evangelical Anglicans for the first time. For most American evangelicals teetotalism was virtually part of the gospel package. These evangelical Anglican clergy all drank good sherry. The Anglican evangelicals must have wondered about the credentials of this group of Americans. The combination of expensive suits, watches and jewellery might have been a little hard for the world-denying, poverty-stricken Anglican clergy to take in. From the very different perspectives of both groups, the other side must have seemed worldly indeed!

The impact of the Graham crusades was impressive. More than two million people attended the twelve-week crusade and over 36,000 decisions were recorded. British evangelicalism had not seen anything on this scale since the days of Moody and Sankey. This single event helped to boost the growing sense of confidence amongst evangelicals. At a very practical level it also helped to boost the number of ordinands in many denominations but particularly in the Church of England. This increase in candidates coincided with a growth in the number of evangelical theological colleges that were available to train them.

The general resurgence in evangelical numbers was further helped by a number of organisational developments. In 1955 John Stott formed the influential Eclectic Society for Anglican evangelical clergy under the age of forty. In 1960 the Anglical Evangelical Council was founded. This organisation held two important congresses, one at Keele in 1967 and one in Nottingham in 1977. These pivotal events were useful measures of the progress of evangelical Christianity since the dreary days of the 1930s.

Other evangelical groups in the major historic denominations learned from the Anglicans and have followed similar strategies in working to change the course of their influence in their respective denominations. Although the relative strength of evangelicals in each of the larger historic denominations varies considerably, some progress in terms of organisational strength, size and number of evangelical congregations, appointments within denominational ecclesiastical structures and teaching appointments in denominational colleges has begun to reflect something of the growing numbers, vibrancy and confidence of evangelicals. Combined with the dramatic growth of smaller denominations which are strongly identified with the evangelical cause, the point has almost certainly been reached in Britain where the definition of where the mainstream of Christianity actually lies is being reworked for the first time since the rapid demise of the evangelical cause in the 1920s.

In the United States, that point was reached some years ago. The strategy of evangelicals there has been markedly different from that in Britain. The impact of the withdrawal of the fundamentalists in the 1920s has meant that there has been a lesser attempt on the part of evangelicals to influence the historic denominations in the way that has taken place in Britain. Instead, there has been a constant and sometimes dramatic growth of those denominations which are either conservative evangelical or Pentecostal in character. The pan-evangelical alliance which was fostered by the decision in the 1940s to include Pentecostals in the evangelical family was of immense importance. The influence and size of Pentecostal denominations, combined with the emergence of the charismatic movement of the mid 1950s and 1960s, has produced a total constituency that is considerably larger than anything that the earlier fundamentalism would have been likely to command. One particular reason for this has been the ability of Pentecostalism to grow and develop amongst the black community, within which some scholars argue it began, and to move beyond the white Anglo-Saxon community (so important to the fundamentalists) by building large followings in the increasingly important Hispanic community.

This growth, combined with the decline of the historic and more liberal denominations has produced a new religious consensus in the United States. The presence of a shift in the religious mainstream began to be noticed as early as the 1970s. Its recognition by society as a whole was highlighted by the successful candidature of Jimmy Carter as President of the United States in 1976. Ironically, Carter himself was never particularly dependent on an evangelical lobby but his personal religious stance brought the issue of evangelical, 'born-again' Christianity into the public arena. *Time* magazine designated 1976 as the 'Year of the Evangelical'. A variety of polls since then have shown that a surprising 40 per cent of the total adult American population regard themselves as 'born-again' Christians.

The growth of the evangelical community in Britain and America has been mirrored by an explosion of evangelical support for overseas mission, more particularly on the part of the much stronger American evangelical constituency. At the time of fundamentalist withdrawal most, if not all, of the major missionary organisations were left in the hands of denominations which were adopting a more liberal stance. The position since then has gradually shifted to reflect a new dominance in mission by evangelicals.

It has been suggested that in the early 1920s North American Protestant missions supported some 14,000 missionaries. By the middle of the 1980s, there were some 39,000 career missionaries supplemented by nearly 30,000 short-term workers. Approximately nine out of ten of this total missionary force were evangelicals not affiliated to the old-line denominational missionary boards.[4] These evangelical missionaries have hardly been affected by the crisis of confidence in missions experienced so powerfully by the older denominations.

The adoption by Edinburgh 1910 of a call to evangelise the world has been taken up by the evangelical constituency. The statistician David Barratt estimates that the late 1980s and early 1990s have seen 1145 plans by mid 1995 designed to evangelise the world by the year 2000. All of these plans come from the evangelical community.

The explosion of interest in mission on the part of the new evangelicals has been accompanied by the dramatic growth of indigenous churches in the two-thirds world which share a common agenda with Western evangelicals. The effect has been to shift the predominant style of world Christianity to an even greater extent than that which has taken place in the

West. The global dominance of evangelicals can now be seen in such places as the Anglican communion. The meeting in Canterbury of Anglican bishops from around the world in 1988 gave rise to calls for a new urgency in evangelism. African bishops were foremost in calling for initiatives which gave rise to the adoption by the Anglican church in England of the Decade of Evangelism. The idea that evangelicals world-wide are helping to set the agenda for the church in the West comes as an entirely new experience for a whole generation of church leaders.

Although the precise strategies and flavour of the evangelical renaissance differ from country to country, there are certain common and recognisable themes which help to identify evangelicalism as a single movement. First, the earlier anti-intellectualism of fundamentalism is now absent. The idea that a rather narrow form of the Christian faith, and along with it the Bible, has to be defended against the attacks of the world has been largely abandoned. It is not that evangelicals now share with liberals an agenda of accommodating the Christian faith to the world; far from it. The adoption by evangelicals of a more positive attitude towards such matters as biblical criticism has enabled them to use scholarship to identify the weaknesses of such a method and to attempt a redefinition of what biblical scholarship might produce. As Derek Tidball has pointed out, even the question of hermeneutics was 'discovered' by evangelicals at the Anglical Evangelical Congress at Nottingham in 1977,[5] a position which would have been unthinkable within fundamentalism.

Second, in parallel with this new intellectual confidence, evangelicals have attempted to engage with contemporary culture rather than to hide from its vicissitudes in a separatist world. Theologians such as Francis Schaeffer, along with many others, have sought to understand the thinkers and intellectual movements which have taken Western society away from Christian values. Instead of offering a 'come out from among them' approach to culture, evangelicals have tried to develop a critique of modern culture that can affirm some developments and attempt to demonstrate the relevance of Christian faith to the contemporary world. In such a climate men like C. S. Lewis have become evangelical heroes.

Third, the tendency of fundamentalism to look at any social concern as akin to preaching a 'social gospel' has been replaced, as evangelicals have attempted to take the social implications of the gospel far more seriously. Evangelicals in Britain contribute significantly to overseas aid through the creation of agencies such as TEAR Fund (The Evangelical Alliance Relief Fund). American evangelicals have created a number of such agencies, notably World Vision. Although the position in the United States is somewhat complicated by an increasingly rightward shift in political allegiance, in general terms evangelicals across the world are demonstrating both a compassion for needy people and an awareness that unjust political and social structures need to be changed. In Britain, a large number of projects that cover a range of concerns from political lobbying to practical help amongst the homeless, drug addicts, AIDS sufferers and the unemployed have proliferated in recent years.

Fourth, the isolation of fundamentalists not only in relation to culture and scholarship but also in relation to other Christians has been ended by the activity of the new evangelicals. It is not that such thinking has disappeared altogether, but where it does exist it is a minority position. In England this particular issue surfaced in dramatic fashion in the 1970s with the call of Martyn Lloyd-Jones for evangelicals to leave the historic denominations and form a 'pure' evangelical church. Lloyd-Jones was somewhat influenced in this stance by developments within Congregationalism, which at that time was preoccupied with discussions on union with the English Presbyterians. Lloyd-Jones was very dismissive of the church which emerged from these negotiations — the United Reformed Church, reputedly calling it neither united, nor reformed nor a church. But his polemical call did not reflect the dominant trend amongst evangelicals and was firmly rejected by Anglican evangelicals to whom it was primarily directed. Since this time there has been a tendency for the more Reformed evangelicals to stand a little on the edges of evangelical activity, especially because of their unhappiness with the broader evangelical alliance with Pentecostals and Charismatics (although this latter concern was not shared by Lloyd-Jones). The early years of the 1990s have seen some efforts amongst evangelicals in the Reformed tradition both to revitalise their own tradition and to build bridges more broadly with evangelicalism. One example of this move has been the creation of the Proclamation Trust which has recently sponsored a week within the wider Spring Harvest celebration.

The overall effect of this new evangelical renaissance has been to produce a reforming, confident, concerned evangelical movement which in many respects has the same flavour as the late nineteenth-century evangelicalism that both acted as the powerhouse for mission and laid the groundwork for Edinburgh 1910. The last twenty-five years have seen the emergence of a world-wide network of evangelicals that is both thinking and acting on a global scale. As in the previous century, the dominant motivation behind such networking is that of evangelical concern for mission in all its forms.

Evangelical global networking

Foremost in promoting the evangelical concern for overseas mission, the Inter-Varsity Christian Fellowship began holding missionary conferencs for students every three years in America. The first of these gatherings took place in 1946, and by 1970 the Urbana conference attracted as many as 20,000 students. The Urbana conferences helped to set the scene for an International Congress on World Evangelization to be held in Lausanne in 1974. The intention of this event was to enable a genuine world dialogue between Western and Third-World Christians on the subject of the evangelization of the world. The international networks of leaders such as Billy Graham and John Stott, together with links formed through the World Evangelical Fellowship were important ingredients in drawing together a very representative gathering of leaders from around the world. The contribution of evangelicals from Latin America was crucial in terms of bringing the issue of the social implications of the gospel onto the agenda of missionary concern.

The final document produced by the Congress included these words: 'The message of salvation implies also a message of judgement upon every form of alienation, oppression, and discrimination, and we should not be afraid to denounce evil and injustice wherever they exist.'[6]

The Lausanne Covenant from which this statement is drawn included a ringing call to enter into a solemn covenant to work with God and with others for the evangelisation of the world. The Lausanne Congress gave rise to what has become known as the Lausanne movement, which has helped to generate both national and international networks of evangelicals concerned to work together in world mission. The momentum that flowed from Lausanne was not unlike that which flowed from Edinburgh and which gave rise to the International Missionary Council earlier in the century.

It resulted directly in a second gathering entitled Lausanne II which was held in Manila in 1989. This event drew together a total of approximately 4300 invited delegates from 173 countries. Unlike the first Lausanne Congress, delegates from Russia and other East European countries were present. Even though the Lausanne movement has faltered somewhat in its direction since 1989, the very gathering itself served as an illustration of the growth, the complexity and the serious intent of evangelicals as a world-wide movement within the Christian family.

Lausanne II helped to generate a number of other initiatives which have since developed practical responses to the challenges of Lausanne at an international level. Two examples of these international networks illustrate current evangelical initiatives.

The first example is the Global Consultation of World Evangelization by the Year 2000 and Beyond (GCOWE '95) held in Korea in May 1995. This event represented an attempt to build collaborative partnerships as a means of taking advantage of the evangelistic opportunities presented by the last decade of this millenium.[7] Prior to the conference, the organisers pointed to seven characteristics of GCOWE.

1. **An assessment of the unfinished task.** Essentially, this represented an attempt to draw together the best possible information on unreached peoples together with data on how these peoples were being reached.

2. **Prayer for world evangelization.** Although prayer is always an element in the concern of evangelicals, this ingredient represented an attempt to target prayer on specific issues and geographical areas, together with a concern to draw together the various networks for whom prayer represented a special concern.

3. **Grass-roots involvement in every aspect of the process.** The organisers attempted to recruit delegates who were actually involved in the task of evangelism from a list of some 27,000 leaders from around the world. In contrast with Edinburgh 1910, if the intentions of the organisers were met, the delegates from Latin America, Africa and Asia vastly outnumbered those from Western Europe and North America.

4. **Mobilizers and practitioners networking together.** The delegates were intended to represent a mix of those who were researching, leading agencies, national church leaders and local leaders.

5. **National strategy development.** The emphasis was on encouraging national Christians to devise strategies for their own nation.

6. **A major Korean role.** The location of the congress in Korea was seen as significant. The leadership of the Korean church in mission was both acknowledged and was also seen as a vital inspirational resource.

7. **Climatic consecration.** The intention of the organisers was to bind delegates and national Christians from Korea in a time of prayer, seen as a time of consecration for the efforts being made in world evangelisation.

The second example is that of the DAWN movement. The title stands for *Discipling A Whole Nation*. The emphasis of the movement is to place church planting at the centre of a strategy for reaching a whole nation. It depends heavily on drawing together Christians of every denomination in a given country in a joint strategy of saturation church planting as a means of evangelising a given nation.

Although DAWN began in an Asian country (the Philippines), it is now being used in countries which belong to the Western world. As such it represents an attempt by evangelicals to work co-operatively for evangelism through a specific but flexible strategy.

These two examples of world-wide evangelical networking stand in contrast to the initiatives that flowed from Edinburgh 1910. Whereas Edinburgh resulted in a significant organisational structure and often began with the historic denominations in Europe and North America, the leadership of much evangelical networking now draws just as heavily from the two-thirds world as it does from the West. These newer evangelical plans rarely result in the creation of large organisations but depend instead on fostering local evangelical networking.

The missiologist Ralph Winter, who was fully involved in planning for the GCOWE '95 event, made an explicit connection between GCOWE and the events leading up to that conference and the Edinburgh conference of 1910.[8] For Winter, the similarity between these two events lay in the commitment to frontier missions as compared with the evangelisation of those nations that already contained a strong Christian community.

Both GCOWE and DAWN represent a sign of the energy of the world-wide evangelical movement at the close of the twentieth century and an indication of possible weaknesses. Although, for understandable reasons, evangelical leaders do not wish to speak in public on this matter, there is a discernible tension between the leaders of Lausanne and those who were responsible for organising both GCOWE and DAWN. The tension lies in the fact that both these latter movements have arguably 'hijacked' many of the key streams found in the Lausanne movement, leaving the Lausanne leaders as interested observers on the sidelines. The tension is felt most acutely in European countries. It is significant that very few denominational leaders from Europe attended GCOWE in Korea. It is arguably the case that few denominational leaders from Korea were consulted or involved in the planning for GCOWE.

This is not the place to record these tensions in detail but the fact that they exist has potential implications for the unity of evangelicals as they come to consider not just frontier missions in the unevangelised world, but the critical task of re-evangelising the Western world. The response of national leaders to this potential division may well be critical as a new century arrives.

Notes

1. For the role of Huxley see Martin Robinson, *The Faith of the Unbeliever*, p. 42.
2. Mark Noll, *A History of Christianity in the United States and Canada*, p. 382.
3. Alister McGrath, *Evangelicalism and the Future of Christianity*, p. 26ff.
4. Joel Carpenter and Wilbert Shenk (eds.) *Earthen Vessels*, p. xii.
5. Derek Tidball, *Who are the Evangelicals?*, p. 51.
6. J. D. Douglas (ed.), 'Proclaim Christ Until He Comes' in *Lausanne II in Manila*, p. 21.
7. Luis Bush, 'GCOWE '95', *Mission Frontiers Bulletin*, May–June 1994, pp. 35ff.
8. This connection is cited and justified in a booklet given to delegates at GCOWE '95 entitled *Thy Kingdom Come: The Story of a Movement* (William Carey Library, Pasadena, 1995).

CHAPTER SEVEN

A NEW WIND BLOWING

Just four years before the delegates gathered at Edinburgh in 1910, an entirely new movement broke out in Los Angeles that was to have a profound impact on the development of world mission. The Pentecostal movement, as it has come to be known, was in its infancy at the time of the Edinburgh Missionary Conference. Hardly any Pentecostal denominations or missionary organisations were in existence by 1910 and although some of the delegates present at Edinburgh from other missionary organisations (notably some from the China Inland Mission) were Pentecostal by experience, these men had not left their denominations to join a Pentecostal denomination; indeed, many of them never did so. In all probability most of those who were present at Edinburgh 1910 would have known nothing of the Pentecostal movement. Certainly the astonishing growth and influence of this movement during the twentieth century could not even have been guessed at by those who were planning missionary strategy.

How can it be that a movement that was not even on the horizon at the beginning of the century can be so important in missions thinking by the end of the same century? At a very basic level, the sheer size and growth of the Pentecostal movement demands some attention. Some have suggested that the Pentecostal movement is not only the fastest growing religious movement of all time, it is also the fastest growing social movement of any kind. The statistician David Barratt estimates that there are some 400 million people in the total Pentecostal family. This approximates to some 25 per cent of the total Christian family.

Even these figures do not fully reflect the impact of the Pentecostal movement because the Pentecostal percentage of the total Christian community varies significantly in different parts of the world. For example, in Latin America, the overwhelming majority of Protestant Christians are Pentecostals. The occasional suggestion that some Latin American countries are developing a Protestant majority could be replaced by asking the question, 'Is Latin America becoming Pentecostal?' It is estimated that in East Asia, Pentecostals represent some 80 per cent of all Christians. The growth of Christians in the Pentecostal family in Africa is also very significant. On a global scale, only in Europe can we say that Pentecostals represent an insignificant percentage of the Christian community.

What conclusions might we draw from these variations? One could argue that Pentecostalism has grown fastest in those parts of the world where there is not already a Christian establishment, but this would not be entirely true. For example, one can certainly point to situations in Latin America and the West Indies, amongst others, where Pentecostals have grown significantly in the face of a large established Christian presence. An alternative observation is that Pentecostalism has experienced its greatest expansion in those parts of the world where there is a genuine openness to the Christian message, but has had more difficulty in areas of resistance, such as Europe. This is certainly partly true but still does not tell the whole story. The question that still needs to be asked is this: Has the presence of the Pentecostal message actually contributed to a receptivity to the gospel message in many parts of our world? I want to argue that this is indeed what has taken place and further, that it is this single fact that has helped to reverse the potential decline of the world church seen as a percentage of the world's population. The growth of the Pentecostal movement has above all else been focused on conversion growth as compared with proselytising other Christians or relying on favourable demographic conditions.

A creative genesis

To understand fully how this contribution has been made, it is helpful to reflect a little on some of the features of the Pentecostal movement, many of which were present in the formative early months of its origins as a movement.

1. An intercultural context

The Pentecostal movement began in a largely black American church context. The extent of the genuinely black origins of the Pentecostal movement has been significantly underplayed by many white Pentecostals. In part this may represent a profound ignorance of the history of their own movement on the part of Pentecostals, but certainly in the case of some Pentecostals, for example the early white leader Charles Parham, racism is clearly a factor.[1] The extent of the indebtedness to an initial black leadership was certainly understood by observers who were present in the early years.[2] One such visitor, the Anglican vicar from Sunderland, Alexander Boddy, commented that something extraordinary was taking place because:

> . . . white pastors from the South were eagerly prepared to go to Los Angeles to the Negroes, to have fellowship with them and to receive through their prayers and intercessions the blessings of the Spirit. And it was still more wonderful that these white pastors went back to the South and reported to the members of their congregations that they had prayed in one Spirit and received the same blessings as they.[3]

Nor was this beginning amongst blacks unique to the United States. Much the same process took place in South Africa.

White Pentecostal missionaries arrived in South Africa in 1908 and went first to the black community. The first Pentecostal meetings in that land took place in a 500-strong congregation of Zulu people in the slum district of Doornfontein in Johannesburg. Unusual events took place. On one night, fifteen men fell prostrate in a pile in front of the altar. The leader, John Lake, was concerned for the smallest man at the bottom of the pile in case he was suffocated. Later in that same week this small man, whose name was Willum, became the first known Pentecostal in Africa.[4]

The white community made their way to the slums to receive a Pentecostal experience in an African context. The unusual nature of this development was noted by contemporaries:

> Now these men were holding meetings in the slums, and in a native church, I had never been in these slums before and never in a large company of natives, imagine with what fear and trembling I accompanied the others. Every minute I expected to be murdered.[5]

> . . . then we heard that two men were preaching Pentecost in the slums of Doornfontein, so I asked Hubby to take the children and go and find out all about it, and they all came home somewhere near two o'clock in the morning. The first thing they said was 'Oh Mammie, Daddy was sitting all in between the coloured people and he said that the clock was going round too fast!' I said, 'Well then this must be of God, because I knew he always hated the natives.'[6]

The later development of the Pentecostal movement in both black and white communities became separated. In South Africa that separation did not happen quite as quickly as in the United States. The separation often meant that the significance of the black Pentecostal movement was not fully understood by the white Pentecostal churches. For example, the Assemblies of God has often claimed to be the largest Pentecostal denomination in the world and this claim has

often been repeated by those outside the Pentecostal movement as an objective fact. Actually there is a black-led
denomination, the Church of God in Christ, that claims to
be twice the size of the Assemblies of God.

Leaving aside these significant misunderstandings, the
essential point about black Pentecostalism both in the United States and elsewhere is that its leadership has always
been black and its development has enabled it to play a
critically important role in the wider black community. For
example, in the United States the Church of God in Christ
has provided an important avenue of advancement for the
black business community. The self-help black employment
schemes of that church have led to the creation of many
significant black businesses and leaders. The freedom
marches of Martin Luther King would probably not have
succeeded without the help of the black Pentecostal
churches. These churches provided accommodation and
food for the marchers in every city and town that they
passed through.

2. Indigenous expression

As this early history suggests, part of the genius of Pentecostalism lies in its ability not merely to thrive in an intercultural context, but also quickly to assume an indigenous
expression. Some of the earliest examples of the growth of
Pentecostalism in the Latin American context clearly display
both an intercultural formation and an early indigenisation,
sometimes out of sheer necessity.

The Brazalian Pentecostal movement began as a result of
the work of two Swedish Baptists. Gunnar Vingren and
Daniel Berg arrived in Belem, in the north of Brazil in
November 1910. On the way they had spent a short time in
the United States. After a brief time with a Baptist congregation, their insistence on preaching a Pentecostal message led
to a division. By 1911 they had established the first Brazilian
Pentecostal church. Since at this time they still had a limited

knowledge of Portuguese, they were forced to rely on Brazilian co-workers. Their own role lay more in inspiring the Brazilians by their own dedication and commitment. As one Pentecostal historian puts it: 'Their efforts rapidly produced a church that lay well beyond their own energies and resources, as they early transferred responsibilities to Brazilian leadership capable of extending the work indefinitely.'[7]

By 1930 this single Pentecostal denomination had attracted 60,000 adherents. In 1969 the Swiss sociologist, Lalive d'Epinay, argued that Pentecostalism in Chile, in contrast with other North American Protestant missionary work, was 'the only form of Protestantism that was authentically South American'.[8] Similar patterns can be demonstrated in many other parts of the world.

However, there have been cases where Pentecostal missions from the West have experienced similar results to those of other Western missionary organisations. In these cases there has usually been a failure to recognise and involve indigenous leadership at an early stage. The attempt to exercise too much missionary control has led to situations where the Pentecostal message has left the mission and new indigenous Pentecostal denominations have been established with no foreign missionary involvement. This has sometimes taken place even when the work has been subject not so much to missionary control as to control from social and cultural groups that have been alien to those who were being reached. The Apostolic Faith Mission of South Africa is one outstanding example of this process. The growth of the indigenous groups that establish their own Pentecostal works has always tended to far exceed the original missionary work.

3. The contribution of the laity

The role of lay people in the Pentecostal movement is vitally important in three closely related areas, first, that of witness. Pentecostalism arose in the context of the holiness revival movement, which in turn was descended from the earlier Methodist holiness tradition. A key component of this stream of Christian spirituality is that of the experience of crisis. The initial crisis experience may be that of conversion itself. Both Pentecostal and holiness groups exhibit a wide range of theologies concerning experiences of sanctification and/or Spirit baptism subsequent to that of conversion. But whatever the precise formulation, the experience of some kind of dramatic crisis forms a common part of Pentecostal expectation.

The normal response to a dramatic experience, whether that involves dramatic changes in lifestyle or in personal commitment, is to speak about what has taken place. Telling the story of that which has occurred is almost part of the experience itself. Personal witness to others on the part of every believer is a normal part of the Pentecostal expectation. It is this use of ordinary believers to bear witness and indeed to preach outside the worship context that forms such an important part of the growth of Pentecostal churches.

But the contribution of lay people does not end with witness. The role of every believer in the worship experience is vital. Pentecostal worship is not a spectator affair, it is highly participative. Although the exact style and format varies enormously, whether it is in the form of exhortation, prophecy, speaking in tongues, lively and contemporary singing, dancing, the playing of instruments or healing, participation in worship is normal for Pentecostals.

The high degree of participation found in worship is also reflected to a large extent in the leadership styles in Pentecostal churches. Lay people are important in the leadership structure of most Pentecostal churches. There are many leadership roles for lay people; it is in many respects a lay movement. The largest church in the world, the Full Gospel Church in Seoul, Korea has been built largely on the strength of many home-group leaders. These are all lay people.

That does not mean that Pentecostals do not also have a

highly authoritarian role for their clergy — they often do. But where this exists, the clergyperson is someone who is of and from the people. Indeed he or she may not have had any formal training beyond that which they have experienced in the local church. Even where theological training exists in colleges and seminaries, there is a high value placed on the practical ability of leaders to demonstrate that they can indeed lead. There is one Pentecostal denomination in Latin America that only ordains those who can point to the people whom they have led to the Lord and who now regard them as their pastors. The 'apostolic success' theme as an indication of leadership ability and hence calling is a powerful motif.

4. The demonstration of power

One central conviction is axiomatic for the Pentecostal movement. The Pentecostal experience of 'baptism in the Spirit' makes available to the church the power that seemed to be present in the early church in terms of miracles, exorcism, healing, preaching and understanding the divine purposes of God. That central claim is enormously important in the spread and growth of the Pentecostal movement in most cultures around the world.

The theme of power is of critical importance in the continent of Africa. The cultural anthropologist Charles Kraft worked as a missionary in Nigeria for many years. He was a missionary with a denomination that was not Pentecostal and soon became aware of the importance that Nigerian Christians, in common with other African Christians attach to the issue of the power of the spirit world. He notes: 'We went out with training in biblical studies, anthropology, and linguistics. We were well prepared, except, as it turned out, in the area that Nigerians considered to be the most important — their relationships with the spirit world.'[9]

Kraft goes on to describe his contacts with Nigerian Christians, including their conviction that the greatest problem of the Nigerian people is that of evil spirits. They maintained that spirits 'cause such things as disease, accidents and death, hinder fertility of people, animals and fields, bring bad weather (including insufficient rainfall), destroy relationships, harass the innocent and the like'. Kraft comments that both himself and the other missionaries he knew 'were just plain ignorant when it came to spirits'. Pentecostal churches, especially in their indigenous form, are well placed to address just these issues.

Accounts of the dramatic growth of the Pentecostal movement in places as diverse as Brazil, South Africa, Indonesia and China frequently recount that breakthroughs first came with dramatic healings and other unusual events. Indeed, the only parts of the world that do not see the problem of the spirit world as of paramount importance are those places where the Pentecostals are not growing dramatically, namely the secular West, with the possible exception of the United States.

The almost unique example of the growth of the Pentecostal movement in the United States is worthy of note. The early conclusion of many observers of the Pentecostal movement was that it was the religion of the dispossessed. This view is certainly borne out by the experience of Pentecostalism in the United States. Blacks, Hispanics, poor whites, immigrant groups of many kinds, and those in the South who felt dispossessed by a dominant 'Yankee' North were all major contributors to the early and continued growth of the Pentecostal movement in that land. There are some similar trends in Europe. One of the largest Pentecostal movements in Europe has taken place amongst one of the most dispossessed groups in the continent, the Gypsy community. Gypsy Pentecostals are estimated to make up at least 25 per cent of all the Pentecostals in France. Many others come from the increasingly significant communities of Africans and even of Tamils to be found in Paris and other large industrial cities.

However, merely to relegate the Pentecostal phenonemon in the West to the dimension of meeting the needs of those who are socially dislocated is insufficient to understand the power paradigm represented by the Pentecostal movement. The Pentecostal experience does not merely offer community and belonging, it also speaks of an experience of what we might call subversive hope. Walter Wink helpfully points to the way in which prayer produces a new future. He writes:

> Let us join hands then with faith healers and speakers in tongues. Let us take as allies a few ranters, raving with the vision of a society of justice, health, and love. For intercession, to be Christian, must be prayer for God's reign to come on earth. It must be prayer for the victory of God over disease, greed, oppression, and death in the concrete circumstances of people's lives, now. In our intercessions we fix our wills on the divine possibility latent in the present moment, and then find ourselves caught up in the whirlwind of God's struggle to actualise it.[10]

The Pentecostal movement has not offered an experience of escape from a harsh world so much as a vision of a changed world. Its message has been of the empowerment of ordinary people in order to bring liberation, personal dignity and hope. That message suggests that the sensory world, which a secular world view claims is the only real world, is merely part of the story. Beyond that which is immediate and material lie forces of good and evil which can help to shape the future for good or ill. The Pentecostal message seeks to align ordinary, powerless people with the power, proclamation and demonstration of the kingdom of God. The Pentecostal experience of 'baptism in the Spirit' enables believers to enter into that new power paradigm.

That paradigm makes a great deal of sense to the majority of cultures in our world but the modern secular world has proved to be highly resistant to such a suggestion. However, there would appear to be some significant cracks in the structure of modernity.[11] Increasingly the post-modern world which is beginning to make itself felt in relation to modernity offers a new openness to the kind of message that the Pentecostal experience brings. Europe in particular and the secular West in general may well be a future mission field which is highly receptive to a Pentecostal spirituality.

Fresh winds blowing

The early Pentecostals saw their movement as one which would renew the existing churches. It was understood as a revival similar to that of the Great Awakening of the Midwest in America or the Welsh revival of 1904 which would bring new life to the existing Christian church. In Britain and elsewhere it was seen as offering a dynamic new resource for overseas missions. However, it soon became apparent that the Pentecostal message was not welcome in the overwhelming majority of churches and Pentecostal denominations soon appeared.

This early period in Pentecostal history was marked by considerable controversy. In Britain the activities of Pentecostals in their annual convention in Sunderland often attracted the attention of the more sensational elements of what we would call today the tabloid press. Large pictures of people dressed in what look like striped pyjamas being baptised in the North Sea gave the feeling that these people stood on the religious fringe. The controversy which was often whipped up by the secular press was given added bite by the degree of hostility and condemnation that flowed from other Christians, notably amongst the holiness groups from which many of the first Pentecostal participants came. It hardly seemed likely that the wider church would look to such an extreme fringe for renewal and inspiration.

The isolation of the early Pentecostal movement was an important factor in helping to define their own self-understanding as distinct from all other Christians. Many early leaders recount tales of having stones thrown at their buildings while worship took place. When your meeting place has a galvanised tin roof, as many Pentecostal halls did, the effect of stone throwing is all the more difficult to ignore. The common memory of persecution made it difficult for Pentecostals to even think of developing constructive and practical working relationships with other Christians. This sense of being separate meant that Pentecostals often tended to exhibit the very sectarian attitudes that their opponents used as a means of justifying their hostile attitude towards the Pentecostal movement. As recently as 1954 the standard evangelical work in Britain on 'Christian deviations' listed the Pentecostals as a cult.

In the United States the organisation that preceded the National Association of Evangelicals had refused to allow any Pentecostal groups to join. But in 1943 a few Pentecostal denominations did join the National Association of Evangelicals. This significant development heralded a growing change, with Pentecostals beginning to be associated with the broader evangelical community. But even with this new acceptance, the dominant tendency amongst Pentecostals by the midpoint of the twentieth century was to see the Pentecostal movement as synonymous with the Pentecostal denominations. To receive a Pentecostal experience inevitably meant to leave your existing denomination and join a Pentecostal denomination. The text 'come you out from among them' was certainly one of the better known texts among Pentecostals.

This first phase of the Pentecostal movement is usually referred to as classical Pentecostalism and many of the sociological studies that refer to Pentecostalism as the religion of the dispossessed accurately describe this first phase of the movement. However, later developments began to make it clear that this was not an adequate description of the movement that is now called the Pentecostal–Charismatic movement. Even in the 1950s it was becoming clear that the classical Pentecostal denominations were having difficulty in knowing who was truly part of the movement and who was not.

In 1947 the Pentecostals organised the first World Conference of Pentecostal Churches in Zurich. Soon after this first conference, David du Plessis became the energetic Secretary of the World Conference. Two other World Conferences took place, in Paris in 1948 and in London in 1951. Both these events were also unsuccessful in understanding the full extent of the Pentecostal movement. The larger Pentecostal denominations had difficulty in recognising some developments as legitimate parts of the Pentecostal movement. To some extent this was simply because some of the activities of the healing evangelists seemed to be rather extreme at that time, and the more established Pentecostal denominations had only just succeeded in achieving a degree of recognition from other evangelicals. The so-called Latter Rain movement was clearly Pentecostal in character but it often condemned the older Pentecostals for being insufficiently Pentecostal. In countries outside the West, other indigenous movements were developing, but because some of these had left the parent Pentecostal missionary body, there was a reluctance to see them as part of the Pentecostal family.[12]

If these difficulties were not enough, by the mid 1950s reports began to appear saying that some in the traditional mainline churches were experiencing the 'baptism in the spirit'. While one might have expected that under normal circumstances Pentecostals would have been delighted to see such developments, there was one significant problem. These new recruits to the Pentecostal experience opted not to follow the well-worn path of leaving their existing churches and either joining an existing Pentecostal church or starting another. These neo-Pentecostals, as they were first called, presented a significant problem to the classical Pentecostal denominations.

The controversy centred on the activity of David du Plessis

who not only ministered to those in the mainline churches but actually recommended to Baptists, Methodists, Episcopalians and others that they should stay in their churches. Moreover, he used his connections with denominational leaders to ask that those (especially ministers) who were receiving the baptism of the Spirit should be permitted to remain within their churches. Du Plessis was beginning to build extensive contacts with the ecumenical movement and especially with the International Missionary Council. He was invited to attend the second World Council of Churches Assembly at Evanston, Illinois in 1954 and continued to attend every succeeding Assembly until his death in 1987.

Although originally from South Africa and a former General Secretary of the Apostolic Faith Mission in that land, du Plessis was a recognised minister with the Assemblies of God in the United States during the time that he was developing what he called his ministry to 'Pentecost outside of Pentecost'. The leaders of a number of evangelical denominations who were strongly opposed to any contact with non-evangelical churches and especially with any form of ecumenical activity began to complain to the leaders of the Assemblies of God about du Plessis' activities. Eventually he was disciplined by the denomination, and because he refused to cease his contact with Christians in ecumenically aligned churches his credentials as a minister were withdrawn.

By the time that du Plessis was disciplined by the Pentecostals, it was already clear that a new movement, soon to be called the Charismatic movement, had begun. Despite some exceptions to the general rule, especially in the United States, most of those who identified with the Charismatic movement in the early days were clearly from the evangelical fold. But this early pattern began to change as those in other traditions, including the Roman Catholic church, began to embrace a charismatic experience. Echoing the first Pentecostals, the initial conclusion of Charismatics was that this new movement heralded an imminent revival, first in the church and later beyond the church.

The expectation of the outbreak of revival produced by this 'second wind' as some also called it, was not to be fulfilled. What came instead was a succession of other waves of the Pentecostal–Charismatic movement. The early 1970s saw a new development in the Charismatic movement. The 'House Church' movement advocated a withdrawal of Charismatics from the mainstream churches. God was doing 'a new thing'. The hope of those in the House Church movement was that revival was now taking place outside the churches. The House Church movement was itself followed by further 'waves' of charismatic activity. Some described the development of networks such as the Vineyard churches of John Wimber as a 'third wave'. Still others claim to have recognised a 'fourth wave' of renewal and so on. The early 1990s saw the expectation that a new outbreak of revival was imminent. Some have claimed that the 'Toronto blessing', widely reported in the summer of 1994, represented an early manifestation of this revival. Whether this turns out to be true or not, it clearly points to the likelihood of many more such 'waves' giving added momentum to the movement.

The creation of new 'House Church' networks might have been expected to mirror the development of the older Pentecostal denominations. But despite every expectation that this is what might take place, recent history has revealed a rather different pattern. Some remarkable alliances within and across the various streams of charismatic renewal suggests that the fruit of the Pentecostal–Charismatic movement may indeed transcend the mere creation of yet more denominational groupings. What might be happening is the birth of a stream within the Christian family which stands beside the older Catholic and Protestant traditions and which is helping to redefine the essence of the Christian experience itself.

A new spirituality

Not long after the 1948 Amsterdam Assembly of the World Council of Churches, Lesslie Newbigin gave a series of lectures that were largely in response to the contribution made by Karl Barth at that meeting. Newbigin's lectures were published as a book entitled *The Household of God*. A great deal of Newbigin's approach was influenced by his own experience of mission and leadership within one of the emerging young churches in Asia. Newbigin suggested that the growing ecumenical movement had allowed a reassessment of the contributions of the two great streams within Christianity — the Catholic and Protestant streams. The one laid emphasis on given structure, the other on the given message of the Christian faith. Both could help each other. However, Newbigin could not help feeling that these two streams somehow failed to encompass the whole of Christian tradition. Looking at church history he saw another tradition. It was one which he found hard to name but he knew that although sometimes it agreed with the Catholic stream more than the Protestant stream and vice versa, it was quite distinct from the other two streams. He wrote: 'For want of a better word to use in this connection I propose to refer to this type of Christian faith and life as the Pentecostal.'[13]

At this particular time, Newbigin was unaware of the existence of Pentecostal churches and he was not referring to the Pentecostal denominations so much as a deeper stream within the history of the church. Actually, those Pentecostal leaders who read his words, particularly David du Plessis, did not realise that he was not writing directly of the Pentecostals and mistakenly but helpfully took great encouragement from his words. Yet, without realising it, Newbigin may well have been describing the development of a stream of Christianity which, although it is no longer identified entirely with the Pentecostal denominations as such, has developed and grown as a direct result of their witness.

Newbigin was seeking for an expression of the faith that would end the false antipathy of message and structure by adding that dimension of the Spirit which brings life and unity to the other two dimensions of Christianity. It might have been difficult to recognise the Pentecostal movement in the first half of the twentieth century as a harbinger of such a dimension. It seemed all too often that Pentecostalism merely introduced more sectarian strife instead of the power to bring unity and a broader life within the whole church.

But the second half of the twentieth century has revealed a different picture. The key to that change arrived with the perception that the Pentecostal movement was defined by an experience and not by a doctrine. Although he was not alone in making such a suggestion, David du Plessis was undoubtedly the foremost pioneer of such a conclusion. In 1957 he described how he was aware of thousands of people who were in mainstream churches and who had been 'baptised in the Spirit'. He commented: 'They are in the REVIVAL but have not joined the MOVEMENT. They are PENTECOS-TAL because of their experience and not because of membership in a Full Gospel Church.'[14]

This distinction was a critical one. Before that time the Pentecostal experience was synonymous with a Pentecostal doctrine and a Pentecostal structure. That connection had actually denied the very genius of the Pentecostal Movement itself. The releasing of the Pentecostal experience from a Pentecostal doctrine and structure has allowed the movement to spread far beynd the confines of Pentecostal churches. Its spread has been a vital ingredient in helping to recreate the broadly evangelical alliance of Christians which was so powerful in bringing the first wave of the modern missionary movement into being. It is not that everyone in the newly emerging evangelical coalition is Pentecostal by denomination or experience, but the growing influence of a Pentecostal–Charismatic spirituality has been highly instrumental in building such an alliance. Two stories from a British context serve to illustrate something of this process at a grass roots level.

The first story takes place in a small Nonconformist congregation in central England. For the past fifteen years I have known one small village congregation very well. It is located in a mining village and from 1920 to 1980 its membership hovered consistently between fifteen and twenty members. Over the past several years they have been influenced by a stream of Christian experience made popular by the annual Spring Harvest celebrations. This congregation would not call themselves Pentecostal and certainly none speak in tongues during the Sunday worship. But there is little doubt that the spiritual culture of that congregation has undergone a remarkable transformation. The worship is now lively, even inspiring. There are some members who speak in tongues privately. This is well known in the congregation and is regarded as unexceptional, whereas some years ago it might have produced schism. Attendance at most services has tripled over the past fifteen years. Giving, especially to missions, has increased substantially. Enthusiasm for evangelism, for bold new initiatives, and even for a future church plant abounds. Confidence in the power of the gospel message is fresh and encouraging.

Some years ago I had listened to some older members speak of how things used to be at the turn of the century. They told me that this had been a lively and enthusiastic church. They could easily have been describing the church that now exists rather than the church that used to exist. The believers seem to believe again. This renewed faith and sense of life reflects the fruit of a broader Pentecostal spirituality that has infused many local churches in recent years.

The second story takes place in the life of a large church in central London. The scene is a summer camp organised by

Holy Trinity Church, Brompton. In recent years this church has been regarded as a leading evangelical and charismatic Anglican church. It has played an important part in some of the contemporary movements amongst evangelicals in such matters as church planting. The leaders of this church have helped to bridge-build with the leaders of many of the 'House Churches', now called 'New Churches', and also with overseas leaders such as John Wimber. During the summer of 1994 it was the focus of many secular press reports concerning the 'Toronto blessing'. Lesslie Newbigin was invited to give Bible studies at their summer camp. While he was doing so, many of the 2000 people in the congregation began to be affected by the 'Toronto blessing'. Some were laughing joyously, many others were stretched out on the floor. How would this former Secretary to the International Missionary Council react to such a scene? His first thought was 'these people are drunk'. It didn't take long for a New Testament scholar such as Newbigin to remember that he had heard that phrase somewhere before. The experience he postulated in 1953 as being necessary for the life of the church was being dramatically enacted in a highly respectable Anglican church some forty years later.

These very different congregations are bound together by a single influence which is significantly recasting the shape of the church in the West in the closing years of the twentieth century.

Notes

1. Walter Hollenweger, *The Pentecostals*, p. 23.
2. *Ibid.*, p. 19.
3. Walter Hollenweger, *Pentecost Between Black and White*, p. 9.
4. Martin Robinson, *To the Ends of the Earth*, p. 20.
5. *Ibid.*
6. *Ibid.*

7. Everett Wilson, *Called and Empowered*, p. 74.
8. *Ibid.*, p. 83.
9. Charles Kraft, *Christianity in Culture*, p. 300.
10. Walter Wink, *Engaging the Powers*, p. 10.
11. Martin Robinson, *The Faith of the Unbeliever*, pp. 55ff.
12. Martin Robinson, *op. cit.*, p. 132.
13. Lesslie Newbigin, *The Household of God*, p. 95.
14. Martin Robinson, *op. cit.*, p. 157.

CHAPTER EIGHT

MISSION COMES WEST

The movement of populations from the East to the West stands as a very long-term pattern in human history. Viewed in this way the whole of Europe is merely a peninsula of Asia, a corner of a larger land mass which has conveniently absorbed Asia's surplus population over thousands of years. In successive waves, Celts, Angles, Saxons, Huns, Franks, Vandals, Goths and Visigoths, Lombards and Moors have all journeyed West. The impact of many of these tribes was so great that they gave their names to whole regions and countries in Europe. This constant migration and sometimes conquest from the East has given rise to an ancient fear of Eastern populations. A sense of the potential to be overwhelmed remains part of the European mind-set. It does not seem to occur to the nations situated to the East of Europe that large numbers of people from the West might want to migrant in an eastward direction.

This has happened on a small scale over the centuries, but those who made the journey east were almost always recruited as skilled workers to serve the interests of particular rulers. The German communities attracted by the Russian Czars serve as one example of this smaller migration pattern. The genuine terror that the threat of Ghengis Khan's armies excited in Western Europe some centuries ago reflects something of this ancient paranoia.

The open welcome of the Americas to peoples from

Europe (following the defeat of the native American Indians), stood for a time in stark contrast to the more general European resistance to population movement. From the perspective of European lands burdened by large excess populations the possibility of emigration to the United States in particular acted as a significant safety valve for many European societies. The scale of that migration in the late nineteenth and early twentieth century has given rise to the rather strange situation where there are more Greeks in Philadelphia than in Athens, more Jews in New York than in Jerusalem, more Irish in Boston than in Dublin and so on. Indeed it is estimated that some 44 million Americans claim some Irish descent whereas the whole population of Southern Ireland is only 3.9 million.

But the very scale of migration has now caused the United States and Canada to exercise the same caution felt by Europeans. The stark reality is that the last part of the twentieth century is witnessing world-wide population shifts on a huge scale. These changes are complex matters. In some cases they are simply the result of the move from the land to the city. In other places they are caused by a combination of war and famine. Many minorities feel under racial, political or religious pressure and so desire to emigrate. Still others are motivated by the desire to advance their own life and that of their family in economic terms. Many nations are feeling the pressure of population explosion. Such nations have large numbers of young people, many of whom have expectations of the future that cannot be fulfilled by their own nations. It is much more frequently the young who migrate than the old. The realisation that there is no limit to the number of people who would come to the West from many other areas of the world has caused the barriers to be erected. The old fears of Europe have returned and are now part of the whole story of the West.

But in the meantime some very significant population movements have already taken place, initially because of the demand of European nations for cheap migrant labour. Even though the barriers to further immigration on the same scale have now been raised, that has not ended the growth of these many migrant populations. Most migrant groups have a younger demographic profile than the host community. Their birth rate is significantly higher and even the most draconian of Western immigration laws can hardly prevent the arrival of other close relatives, especially wives and husbands.

The point about these movements is that they have brought large numbers of people to the West who do not share any of the common Western traditions that flowed from the shared experience of Christendom. Their arrival has forced a radical reappraisal of earlier and more liberal assumptions about immigration. That earlier and more benign view believed that immigrants could gradually be absorbed into the general population without too much difficulty. Certainly the first generation and even the second generation would understandably want to retain some links with their homeland. But gradually, inexorably and desirably, integration would take place. There were good reasons for such optimism; earlier examples of this process could be cited. The Huguenots in England, the Scots, Welsh, Irish, Germans, and Scandinavians to name but a few, in the United States. But this happy integration into the general 'soup' of American life and culture overlooked that fact that these many groups had far more in common than they had to separate them. Even the Catholic/Protestant divide was at least a division within a much more ancient stream of common Western culture.

But the more recent arrival of populations who do not share such a cultural inheritance has caused some fundamental questions to be asked about the integrationist model. Many now talk about the hope for a 'stew' rather than a 'soup'. The point about the stew is that while the dish may be common, the ingredients remain distinct and recognisable. But some human history suggests that even the 'stew'

model may prove to be rather optimistic becoming instead a
pressure worker ready to explode. There is cause for believing that many communities are likely to live in entirely
separate streams for generations to come. In such a situation what is at stake is the desire by many minorities to
influence the mainstream of Western life, to challenge it, to
make a place for themselves, and if possible to reshape
Western culture in accordance with their own values and
views.

The missionary growth of other faiths

The past 1000 years of European history have proved to be a
remarkably stable time in terms of large movements of
population by migration alone. The establishment of Christendom and its clear boundaries with the forces of Islam had
the effect of hermetically sealing the populations of Europe
until the discovery of the New World. Until the last forty
years, it was extremely unlikely in practical terms that any
American or Western European would meet someone from
another of the world's major faiths. They could read about
Islam, Hinduism or Buddhism or even receive accounts of
these faiths from missionaries or other travellers, but the
possibility of live contact was almost entirely absent. The
last forty years have brought immense changes to this settled
scene. Certainly there are still many, especially in rural areas,
who have no contact with those of other faiths but as a
society the issue of other faith communities is very much
on the agenda.

Those who travelled to the West as the first generation of
immigrants certainly had no thoughts of converting the West
to their faith. Their priority was the maintenance of their own
faith and that of their families and compatriots. Some may
have doubted whether even this task was possible. They did
not fear Christianity so much as the influence of a secular
society on the thinking of their children. The past twenty

years have demonstrated a considerable success amongst immigrant communities in terms of the establishment of living faith communities in the West. As this process has taken place, the agenda has now changed. The question of winning Westerners to other faiths has gradually become part of a conscious missionary strategy amongst other faith communities.

The three faiths that have been the most able to win converts are Hinduism, Buddhism and Islam. It is not that these are the only faiths which are active in the West. Sikhism, Taoism, and even African tribal and voodoo practices can be found in many cities in the West. But the three major world faiths, Hinduism, Buddhism and Islam, all have a greater presence and a clearer missionary strategy than the variety of other faiths on offer.

1. Hindu missions

The expansion of overtly Hindu worship has come to the West in two major missionary forms. These two forms are listed by the newspaper *Hinduism today* as among the top ten organisatons or individuals that have most influenced Hinduism throughout the world in the 1980s.[1] First, the Hare Krishna sect, more properly known as the International Society for Krishna Consciousness, is probably the most organised and aggressive missionary society amongst the various Hindu groups. The movement was begun by Bhaktivedanta Swami Pabhupada in 1966. Although at times controversial, the movement is recognised by most other Hindus in the West as an authentic expression of Hindu faith. It came to prominence after its founder moved to the United States. In common with a number of other new religious movements, many of the key organisational figures have tended to be Americans. However, despite the fact that Hare Krishna devotees can be seen on the streets of many of the larger cities throughout the West, and now even in many Eastern European cities, their numerical strength is not great. In

Britain the core of full-time devotees of Anglo-Saxon origin is probably no more than a few hundred.

The second major missionary force has been that of the Maharishi Mahesh Yogi and his approach of Transcendental Meditation (TM). According to the Transcendental Meditation's Office of Information and Inspiration, 150,000 people in Britain have taken a four-day course in the technique with a further 6000 people doing so every year. The movement attempts to present itself as a 'scientific' rather than a purely religious movement. This approach has occasionally enabled TM to be presented as an alternative health therapy rather than an alternative religious system. In recent years, the TM organisation has launched a political party in Britain. One suspects that the motivation is not so much an attempt to gain political power as to use the opportunity for publicity. The party, known as the Natural Law Party, fielded a candidate in every constituency in the 1992 General Election in Britain. It also distributed an eight-page broadsheet newspaper to every home in Britain in support of its candidates and fielded candidates for every constituency in Britain during the 1994 European Elections.

2. The spread of Buddhist witness

As with all other major religions, there are a number of forms of Buddhism operating as a missionary faith in the West. One form, Nichiren Shoshu Buddhism, began in Japan immediately following the Second World War. It had some 20 million members in 115 countries by the late 1980s.[2] Nichiren Shoshu in America was founded in 1960. The first members were nearly all the Japanese brides of American servicemen. By the mid-1970s, they claimed 200,000 adherents of whom some 20,000 were not originally from the Far East. The movement came to Britain in 1974 through the efforts of an Englishman who had been converted while in Japan. Today the organisation in Britain claims some 4000 members.

3. The growth of Islam

For many Muslims, the years of colonial domination by the Western powers represented a puzzle. Their expectation had always been to see Islam as missionary and expansionary. Today, Islam around the world has recovered a measure of confidence. World mission is once more on the agenda for Islam. The three factors of oil money, the movement of large numbers of Muslims to areas of the world which have traditionally been unaffected by Islam and the emergence of newly independent nations with a self-consciously Islamic identity have helped to fan the flames of missionary enterprise.

Many Islamic leaders have spoken of the goal of converting the West to Islam. Because, unlike many other religions, Islam is a total social, political and religious system, such a goal inevitably has a political dimension. Although it is true that the mere setting of a goal is not the same thing as accomplishing that goal, Muslims have shown some very real commitment to the task of missions thinking. Strategies for winning the West have begun to form. One example of such a strategy is the publication *Islamic Movement in the West*, by Khurram Murad. When this paper was written the author was the Director General of the Islamic Foundation based in Leicester, England. The anti-Western critique offered by Islam is well developed and offers an all-embracing alternative to Western religious traditions. One element of Muslim strategy is to allow specifically Western forms of Islam to develop. There is some evidence that a combination of Western converts together with second- and third-generation Muslim immigrants to the West are beginning to articulate such forms.

In common with other major faiths, Islam is present in the West in a number of guises. Sufism, with its strong mystical element, is possibly proving to be the most flexible and attractive form of Islam as far as indigenous people in the

West are concerned. The overall numbers of converts are not high but they are often drawn from articulate and well-educated sectors of Western society. However, there is one group living within Western society which has responded in significantly large numbers to Islam. The black community, particularly in the United States but also increasingly in Britain, has been successfully touched by Islamic missionary activity. Although Islam is not always anxious to embrace every aspect of this sometimes controversial movement, the high-profile conversion of individuals such as Malcolm X, the boxer Muhammed Ali and even more recently Mike Tyson, have had a growing impact on a population that had formerly been assumed to be almost entirely Christian in its orientation.

The total number of new religious movements coming from outside the West and operating a missions strategy towards Western peoples is considerable. Some, if not all of these groups, have learnt from Western missions activity in their own lands and are merely reapplying the same methods in reverse. However, there are also some important differences between the traditional approach of Christian missions and the strategy of other faiths in relation to the West. Possibly the most important of these differences is that the missionaries from foreign faiths do not come to the West as representatives of cultures and powers that are seeking domination in any colonial sense. Their use of indigenous religious forms and especially of newly converted nationals within the West represents an almost textbook copy of what Christian missions from the West should have done elsewhere and have often failed to do. Strangely, the approach of these faiths often looks more like the spontaneous, frequently lay-led, expansion of the Christian faith, both in the first few centuries, and increasingly over the last few decades in the two-thirds world.

Christian missions to immigrant groups

Despite many years of supporting missionaries to bring the gospel message to peoples of other races and faiths around the world, Christian churches in the West have seemed at a loss to know what to do when representatives of those same peoples come to live next door to their home church. There are few examples of local congregations in the West reaching out effectively to those of other faiths in their neighbourhood.

In the same way, the older missionary agencies have been rather slow to respond to the task of mission in the West. The most common response has tended to be that of 'mission partnership'. This has usually involved bringing clergy from other continents to work in a variety of Western settings. While on occasion this approach has certainly widened the horizon and understanding of Western Christians it has rarely proved to be fruitful as a single strategy in reaching significant numbers of those from other faith communities.

More recent years have seen a number of the more evangelical missions agencies engaging in missionary initiatives amongst immigrant communities. Groups such as Youth With A Mission, Operation Mobilisation and Crosslinks have supported workers solely to work with those of other faiths living in the West. Sometimes these workers have been connected with existing local churches but have spent the majority of their time building relationships with those immigrant peoples that the local churches themselves have been unable to reach. On other occasions these workers have had a goal of planting entirely new congregations composed of converts from other faiths. The limited evidence available so far would seem to indicate a much greater degree of success in winning those from other faiths when the goal is to establish a congregation that worships in a cultural setting that is appropriate for those who are being converted.

It is clear that there has been a steady trickle of converts from Hinduism, Sikhism, Buddhism and Islam to Christianity in a variety of Western countries. But where these converts have had to make the transition to a predominately Anglo-Saxon congregation there has often been a tendency for such converts to fall away. The last ten years has seen an acceleration of the trend for nationals to reach their compatriots across religious divides.

One example of this development can be seen amongst the Tamil people. The Tamil diaspora has reached significant numbers in Britain, Canada, the United States, France and several other Western European countries. These Tamil people come from South India, from Sri Lanka and from parts of the Tamil diaspora in South-East Asia such as Singapore. The civil disturbances in Sri Lanka have caused large numbers of Tamils to come to the West as refugees. Some Tamils were committed Christians before leaving their homeland. As one might expect, the leadership of the various Tamil groups tends to be drawn from the migrating Christians. But the new converts come from a mixture of nominal Christian, Hindu, Buddhist and Muslim backgrounds. The language for worship tends to be Tamil even though there is already some tension between parents and those children whose first language increasingly comes from the West.

There is every likelihood that the strategy of nationals reaching their own people will prove to be a much more effective means of reaching the significant numbers of migrants who are coming to live in the West. In those situations where Christian leadership cannot be found amongst immigrant groups, the first goal of mission will need to be to establish such a leadership rather than to expect cross-cultural missionaries to be primarily responsible for reaching large numbers of people themselves.

The impact of Christian immigrants

Apart from the arrival of large numbers of immigrants from other faith communities, there are many examples of the arrival of similarly large numbers of immigrants who come from lands which already have a predominantly Christian faith and culture. Christians from the West Indies and from parts of Africa have travelled to some Western lands, especially to those countries which have had colonial links with such nations. Some of the largest congregations in a number of Western cities are composed entirely of people from other lands who arrived as Christians. One of the largest Protestant congregations in Paris consists of Christians from Zaire. Whereas many Christians from overseas believed they were coming to live in a predominantly Christian country, it is often those from Zaire and not from France who travel on the Metro on a Sunday morning, smartly dressed and carrying a large black Bible.

The impact of these migrating Christians has been complex and thus difficult to understand. We have to face the fact that not all of those who arrived as practising Christians remained so after their arrival. It is estimated that of those West Indians who came to Britain in the 1950s and 1960s, some 90 per cent had been regular church attenders before leaving those islands. Within ten years of arriving in Britain only 30 per cent were still attending a church. The bleak experience of racism both within and outside the churches formed part of the reason for this exodus. Of those who continued to attend, approximately one half continued to attend one or other of the historic white-led churches, with the other half joining one of the many newer black-led Pentecostal churches.

Black Christians, whether from the West Indies or from Africa, have strengthened the total Christian witness, especially in the inner cities. There are those who believe that the activity of black Christians in the inner city has prevented the explosion of tension beyond the occasional eruptions that have already taken place amongst the disaffected young. Such a case is difficult to prove but the high level of imaginative social welfare schemes undertaken by black Christians must have made some difference to the dignity and self worth of the many thousands of black young people who have attended them.

The childen of those black Christians are beginning to make their witness felt in areas well beyond the inner city itself. Increasing numbers of second- and third-generation immigrants are now making their witness in the professions, in parachurch agencies and to a small extent in the denominational leadership of the historic churches. My personal experience of working in the inner city suggests to me that the frequently enthusiastic and yet doctrinally conservative faith of black Christians has often caused Anglo-Saxon Christians to reconsider the claims of their own faith in a thoroughly helpful manner. These thousands of unpaid missionaries have been able to assist in the regeneration of the church in precisely those places where Christian witness has been weak.

Yet the combined effect of frustrated hope, racism, family breakdown and the secularism of the West has often meant that younger blacks have become increasingly distanced from Christian churches of all kinds. First the Rastafarian movement and more recently the Black Muslim preachers have had a cultural, even if not yet an entirely religious impact, on many young blacks. These more recent developments suggest that a new and difficult mission field is opening up amongst those members of the black community born and brought up in North America and in Western Europe.

Mission from the two-thirds world to Anglo-Saxons

The newspaper headline put it bluntly, 'Missionaries fly in to save godless Britons'.[3] The idea that churches overseas might be sending missionaries to countries such as Britain is still newsworthy, which implies that it is also out of the ordinary. The numbers involved in coming as missionaries to the West are not yet vast, but such a development forms part of the changing reality of a world-wide church.

We have already noted that some missionary societies and denominations in the West have adopted a policy of bringing clergy as 'mission partners' to Britain. But this fairly low key approach to cross-cultural mission is increasingly being supplemented by missionaries who are not brought in by the church in the West but who are sent by the church elsewhere. This often means starting from no base at all. The newspaper headline quoted above tells the story of Sung Hee Kwon from South Korea:

> She left her high-flying job with a bank in Seoul to come to south London in 1985, she spoke only a few words of English. Initially she gave out leaflets on the streets of Streatham and talked to people walking in the parks. Now Sung, who converted from Buddhism 19 years ago, has up to 70 people in her Christian worship groups.

Such progress, undramatic as it may seem, is actually fairly remarkable. The experience of some missionaries from other continents is often one of bewilderment at the degree of unbelief in the West. The shock of encountering blatant unbelief is often accompanied by the discovery that the forms of worship of the church in the two-thirds world are not easily accepted amongst Anglo-Saxons. The exhortation to join the minister in dancing down the aisle is not received gladly in most Western countries. Certainly the temptation of the two-thirds world missionary is to work only with those immigrants that belong to their own nation. The difficulty of reaching the Anglo-Saxon community is also reflected in the work and witness of the many black-led churches in the West. The leaders of these churches always declare that their intention is not to be a black-only church but to preach the gospel to any who will hear and receive it. I have often asked the leaders of black-led churches if any from the white community have become Christians through the witness of the church. Many if not all can think of some people who have been converted. 'But they don't stay', is the usual rejoinder. What then happens to them? I have also met a number of those white English people who came to faith through the witness of black Christians but who felt unable to stay. It is not a question of racist attitudes so much as feeling culturally alienated within the black-led church.

However, this does raise the question as to how effective missionaries from the two-thirds world are likely to be in the West. Is Sung Kee Kwon from Korea a lonely exception that proves the rule? Until very recently I might have been tempted to think so. But over the last few years I have met enough of these exceptions to believe that such missionaries have a vital and helpful role to play. Let me give one such further example.

The missionary in question comes from Ghana. While in Ghana he worked for a Western oil company in a senior position. He came to Britain to study at a Bible College in order to return to Ghana as a Christian worker. While studying he came to see Britain as a needy mission field and accepted the call to remain as a missionary. After completing his study he travelled a fairly well-worn route within a predominately white-led denomination. He accepted a call to work with a congregation that had some multi-racial membership, but a majority were black. He followed a black West Indian minister who had begun the church. Surprisingly, instead of the church continuing as a largely Afro-Caribbean congregation, they became increasingly composed of white, middle-class, professional members. The congregation now meets in a building rented from the United Reformed Church. The missionary from Ghana is reaching the very people who in former times might have been expected to be part of the church that the building is rented from. It is not possible to say whether the experience of this one individual will be maintained or whether he might eventually find that his congregation begins to attract more and more black members. But even the fact that it has happened for a time represents a significant departure from other earlier patterns.

This progress was preceded by a moment of crisis for our Ghanaian pastor. As he began the task of speaking to the white people in the community he had profound doubts as to how his ministry would be received. His testimony reveals that it was necessary to overcome those severe personal doubts before his ministry began to be effective. Perhaps this moment of personal crisis reflects something of the wider doubts that many engaged in mission in the West have felt. The spiritual resources of his African past were immensely helpful in dealing with such doubt. Does this personal encounter represent something of what the Christian community world-wide might offer to the church in the West? Confidence in the Christian message, its relevance, its efficacy, abounds in the church from China to Peru. This proper confidence is badly needed by a Christian community in the West which feels partly defeated as a consequence of its recent past.

Cross-cultural mission within the West

Although there is evidence of small numbers of European Christian workers serving as missionaries in other European countries, the overwhelming movement of missionaries serving within the West is from the United States to Europe. It is not that the individual work of some European missionaries has not been significant. At least one missionary from Britain is credited with the founding and rapid growth of one of the Pentecostal denominations in France. But the sheer scale of American missionary involvement is such that it requires special attention.

Since the Second World War there has been a steady growth of American missionary involvement in Europe. The war itself had a significant impact on this growth. The sheer number of American servicemen in Europe both during the war and since that time acted to spark an interest in the spiritual future of the continent. Immediately following the war, the initial response of American missions was to offer material relief in the face of the huge refugee problem as Europe faced the massive task of rebuilding its social and political structure. In 1950, as many as sixty three different North American mission agencies were already involved in Europe. By 1990 that number had grown to 187. The number of missionaries serving with these agencies grew from 1971 in 1970 to 3525 in 1979 and 3840 in 1985.[4]

The growth of missions involvement in Europe by North Americans now represents such a significant proportion of personnel and, given the relatively high cost of maintaining missionaries in Europe, an even higher percentage of total financial resource, that the question of the relative success or otherwise of North American missions is of critical importance. At least two detailed studies, both by long-term Baptist missionaries, have been conducted. The first by Allen V. Koop assesses the work of American evangelical missionaries in France from 1945–1975.[5]

Koop's conclusion was that, 'By 1975 the American evangelical missionaries in France realised reluctantly that their growing numbers and their persistent efforts had yielded small results.'[6] He went on to explain the rationalisation offered by the missionaries for this lack of success and notes that the reasons given for their lack of progress did not augur well for the future. His analysis included a survey of the various strategies adopted by missions and comments that the option of partnership with the existing French evangelical community remains the one approach that has been the least favoured. Koop advances the view that this least-used option might turn out to be the most fruitful in the longer term. He offers the depressing explanation that missions'

> . . . primary goal had become not the widespread proclamation of the gospel and Christian ethics, but control of their own converts and churches. They wanted to protect them from liberal or Pentecostal ideas which ran counter to standard evangelical doctrine. Accountability to the home office and to the missionaries' American supporters weighed heavily.[7]

The obsession with control and the related idea of doctrinal purity becomes an all too familiar theme.

The second study by William L. Wagner was written after Koop's work and Wagner had the benefit of being familiar with that earlier study. Wagner's book surveys Protestant missions across Western Europe. He lists the seven areas of work in which the greatest number of personnel are involved. These are:

1. Church planting
2. Personal and small-group evangelism
3. Mass evangelism
4. Literature distribution
5. Broadcasting
6. Theological education
7. Nurture and support of national churches

In attempting to evaluate the success or otherwise of American missions, Wagner makes a detailed assessment of work in just four areas. His major findings are worth noting.

1. Theological education

Wagner notes that in almost every case the theological institutions established by American missions fail to become part of the wider educational system in the host nation. The consequence of this failure is that despite early intentions to become self-financing the institutions become permanently dependent on missions money with all of the tensions that such dependency brings. A related failure is that the expectations of students are often frustrated. Trained students often find that there are no churches to support them once they have graduated. Many schools make the mistake of further isolating themselves by seeking to relate to an American school for accreditation. As Wagner comments, 'In most cases the schools operate in their own orbit and have yet to achieve the status of real European identity.'

2. Church-planting ministries

Wagner points to the influence of church growth strategists such as Donald McGavran who strongly advocated that the creation of networks of new, alive and vibrant local congregations would be a key to the re-evangelisation of Europe. Wagner notes, 'Many missionary societies have taken up McGavran's challenge and made church planting their number one priority. Few have been successful.' The reasons for this failure are many and complex but are all related in one way or another to the inability of missions to set the church-planting effort in the context of local culture. In the area of finance, the level of funding that flows to the missionary cannot be duplicated by a national. The church structures initiated by the missionary only work as long as they are operated by outside funds. It is simply not realistic for European workers to be asked to operate a structure that represents a cultural imposition if they are to raise funds for that purpose within the culture. Unfortunately, that is precisely what the small number of European converts have come to expect of the European worker. Wagner comments:

> The result of many years of church planting is a weak, fragmented network of small churches and missions which are seldom self-supporting, much less self-propagating. If the goal has been reached, then one could only evaluate the results as a failure . . . [8]

3. Support ministries for Free churches

Wagner surveys the results of work in a number of European countries where missionaries have worked within the national structures of existing evangelical denominations. He is a little more encouraged by the results of this strategy. He notes that overall, Baptists in Western Europe decreased from 1965 to 1985 by 12.73 per cent. But within that decline, six national Baptist unions grew while ten declined. Wagner attributes the growth in four of the unions to the work of American missionaries.[9] However, despite this more positive evaluation, it is hardly possible to point to any outstanding national successes.

4. Support ministries for State-related churches

The thinking behind this strategy centres on the observation that the overwhelming Christian presence in Europe is either Lutheran, Reformed, Orthodox or Catholic and that all other groups are not taken seriously by many in European society. Therefore renewing these churches has more potential impact than the creation of new denominations or the strengthening of very small ones. This strategy is a relatively new approach and is mostly being adopted by parachurch agencies such as Campus Crusade for Christ. The timescale needed to succeed with this strategy is such that no evaluation can yet take place. To date one cannot point to many success stories.

At first sight, both Koop and Wagner's surveys appear to be very gloomy, especially considering the level of resource that is being expended in the mission field of Europe. However, there are two elements that are encouraging. First, there are some examples of situations where American missions help has been both appreciated and fruitful. These are all situations where dynamic national leaders have emerged and have received help (though almost never personal financial help) from Americans. The most valuable help has been that of friendship, fellowship, occasional mentoring, and the provision of American workers to engage in specific tasks working under national direction. Second, Wagner makes the point that even where ministries such as church planting have so far not yielded the results that might have been expected, the process of indigenisation has begun, which in time may produce the kind of national leadership that will be necessary for significant national movements to develop. There are some indications that this might be happening.

The conclusion therefore is the not-altogether surprising one that the task of re-evangelising Europe will ultimately depend on Europeans. But the work of foreign missionaries, whether from North America or elsewhere can be important along the way. The personal example and inspiration of many missionaries can provide a valuable stimulus to a church which has felt defeated and confused. There are a number of stories beginning to emerge in Europe which reveal that a genuinely intercultural approach to mission can have the effect of stimulating a creative European response.

Notes

1. *World Pulse*, 15 July 1989.
2. Eileen Barker, *New Religious Movements: An Introduction*, p. 193.
3. *Sunday Times*, 21 August 1994, p. 7.
4. William Wagner, *North American Protestant Missionaries in Western Europe*, p. 31.
5. Allen V. Koop, *American Evangelical Missionaries in France 1945–1975*.
6. *Ibid.*, p. 169.
7. *Ibid.*, p. 173.
8. William Wagner, *op. cit.*, p. 182.
9. *Ibid.*, p. 185.

CHAPTER NINE

SIGNS OF HOPE

In his book *The Persistence of Faith* Rabbi Jonathan Sacks writes, 'In recent decades, religion has taken us unawares . . . Instead and against all prediction, religion has resurfaced in the public domain'.[1] The sense that the landscape for the Christian faith in the West might be changing is becoming increasingly widespread. All across Europe and even in parts of North America, the 1960s and 1970s were testing times for the church. Twenty years ago the sheer scale of redundant church buildings in Britain was depressingly visible. Literally hundreds of former chapels and churches could be seen empty, forlorn and for sale. The range of alternative uses as nightclubs, carpet warehouses, garages, factories, shops and occasionally as homes was hardly inspiring. But that depressing phase seems now to be over. There are now signs of hope. The signposts are worth looking at to gain some understanding of the journey that the Christian community is taking. However, as we do so, it is important not to confuse the signposts with the destination. The existence of hopeful signs does not mean that an inevitable return to the Christian faith has begun. The signs represent an opportunity, not a certain outcome.

Cracks in modernity

The widespread disillusionment and hostility in relation to religion in general and towards Christianity in particular which has been such a feature of twentieth-century Europe is showing some signs of abating. At an emotional level, some of this change can be traced to the gradually fading memories of the horrors of war, especially that of the First World War. At an intellectual level significant challenges within the dominant secular establishment are beginning to take place. The fundamental reason for this reconsideration lies in the growing shift that is taking place in our understanding of the way in which the world works. We might call this the 'world-view' adopted by our society. Such world-views are never entirely composed of knowledge alone. The knowledge that we have inevitably comes to us through a number of filters. The metaphors or images that we use to understand our world act both as a means of assimilating information and also as a filter for that information. For example, in order to understand the way in which atoms work we might be encouraged to have an image of billiard balls in our mind. In fact, atoms are not the same as billiard balls, but they are enough like billiard balls in the way they act on each other that such a picture can be a helpful one.

A similar process takes place in relation to the larger pictures that form to allow us to understand such matters as who we are and how we relate to our world. Human beings have normally formed comprehensive explanations of the world, its origins, its purpose and possibly its future in order to help in the process of understanding our own place in the world. For most of its history, the Western world has used the Christian story as a point of reference from which to understand many of these larger questions. The precise details of the story have not been as important as the basic claim that the world has been created by a God who has revealed himself and his purposes to us. Our importance and our future was understood in relation to the coming of Jesus Christ. His life and ministry was seen as the central point of the human story. Time itself was divided by his coming. We speak of events AD and BC. We can call a story or narrative of this significance a 'metanarrative'.

With the arrival of the modern world some aspects of secular thought began to challenge the Christian story. Secularists not only made the claim that the Christian metanarrative was false but that there was a better metanarrative with which to understand the world and our place in it. A number of thinkers, and more importantly a number of popularisers, spread the new story. The secular story claimed that the material, physical world is all that there is. There is no need to resort to the myth that God created the world. The origin of the universe and of life is all explainable by looking at cause and effect. Scientific method is gradually offering an explanation of the whole of the world. The sciences of biology, physics and chemistry are able to demonstrate how the universe has come into being. The disciplines of psychology and sociology are able to tell us why people behave in the way that they do. The story of evolution offers us a grand story, or metanarrative, into which we can fit all of the observable facts that science is revealing. Ethical norms and moral conduct do not come to us from God, they are merely choices which people make in relation to the circumstances in which we find ourselves. The totality of this metanarrative is what we know as modernity.

The hidden proposition of modernity contends that the human race is gradually evolving towards a situation where knowledge will liberate us from the old slavery of ignorance and the world of religious myth. Human, and thus social, progress will gradually end wars, intolerance and every other evil. Technology will put us in charge of our world, even ending the need for labour. At this point man will become 'superman' and the need for God will be ended. God will then, finally, be dead.

However, the more recent experience of mankind has

begun to question this metanarrative. There are now severe doubts that humanity is engaged in an inevitable march of progress. Indeed the fear now exists that we are more likely to be involved in a slow slide towards destruction. The certainty that man will always choose the good is highly questionable. Technology, far from bringing every good gift, is now looked upon as almost out of control. The possible destruction of our world by such diverse means as nuclear holocaust, over-population or the poisoning of our planet are serious threats. Social dislocation as a consequence of the revolution in manufacturing and information technology is bringing as many undesirable consequences as helpful ones.

The world of the physical sciences has also undergone some significant changes. Following the work of Einstein and others, the old mechanistic explanations of the world are slipping away. Physicists are beginning to speculate about the existence of spirit in the world as well as matter. Fresh knowledge is casting doubt on the old certainties of modernity instead of reinforcing them.

This combination of new questioning has helped to produce a philosophical response which some call 'post-modernity'. At the heart of post-modernism lies the claim that the metanarrative of modernity is fatally flawed. It brings a radical pessimism which suggests that not only is the metanarrative of modernity untrue, it is not possible to have any metanarrative by which to explain our world. There is no overarching story which can help us make sense of the universe. There is only a perpetual present which is dominated by our own experience. The only meaning in life is that which we choose to give it. It is as if the world is merely a kind of cruel joke and the only way of engaging with the world is by means of a radical encounter designed to heighten our experience of it.

This rather dark response at least opens the door to a religious dimension in life. The questioning of the modern metanarrative that so strongly opposes a Christian metanarrative offers a new opportunity for Christianity to re-enter the debate about the meaning of our world. However, the gradual questioning of modernity does not mean that there is any easy return to the former Christian metanarrative. It is never possible simply to resurrect the past. The forces of post-modernity are actually opening the door as much to what we might call neo-paganism as to Christian belief. But at least a new stage for Christian proclamation is beginning to present itself.

At a popular level this new openness manifests itself as a readiness to talk about religious issues. Although difficult to document, there would seem to be sufficient anecdotal evidence to suggest that spirituality, even if it comes in guises other than formal religious systems, constitutes part of a changing cultural landscape. John Drane, Director of the Centre for Christianity and Contemporary Society at the University of Stirling tells a number of such stories in a recent book. He quotes the actress Joanna Lumley as saying, 'In the 1990's we're going to start finding our souls again.'[2] Drane then records this astonishing story:

> Not long ago, I gave an address in one of Britain's most ancient universities. It was about the so-called 'New Age' phenomenon, and after I spoke the person chairing the meeting (which was part of a Christian mission) asked for questions and comments. A man in his forties jumped up right away: 'I am a professor of chemical engineering,' he said, 'but I've been a wizard for the last fifteen years, and I'm thinking about becoming a Christian.' The chairperson was lost for words! The combination of being a university professor, a wizard and a potential convert to Christianity was simply mindblowing.[3]

While one cannot pretend that such stories are commonplace, in my own travels I have met enough new Christians converted from completely unchurched backgrounds (including a former witch in Denmark) to have gained the strong sense that we are entering religious waters which have been uncharted in the West during recent years.

Changing church

However, as John Drane also comments, we should not assume that these changes in the culture should automatically be read as good news for the church.[4] A great deal depends on how the church responds to the emerging situation. Drane argues that the church is severely weakened by its own identification with modernity. This has left many Christians unsure how to respond to the new situation as represented by a growing interest in spirituality. It has also caused institutional Christianity to be perceived as totally irrelevant to the new future, even by those who are broadly sympathetic to the Christian ethic.

Over and against this rather pessimistic view of the position of the church, there is growing evidence that the dramatic numerical decline of the church across Europe has ended. This is not the same as suggesting that the church is now experiencing widespread growth: clearly it is not. Indeed, it is still possible to argue that the level of church attendance has sunk so low in many parts of Europe that it has become almost impossible to think of the recovery of the church. In such a scenario Christianity will continue only as the preserve of a minority which stands outside of the major developments in the culture. Closer inspection reveals a more complex picture. Four ingredients in this picture are worthy of notice.

1. A more confident church

First, as we have already suggested in Chapters 6 and 7, the balance of churchmanship has shifted across Europe. The combination of evangelical strength and confidence, together with the growth of the Pentecostal and Charismatic movements and a growing move towards theological orthodoxy on the part of those who do not identify themselves as either evangelical or charismatic, has caused the church to have significantly more confidence in its message. This renewed confidence is not marked for the most part by a desire to return to a cultural ghetto. Far from wishing to retreat from the world in the manner of an earlier fundamentalism, there is a detectable desire to explore the relevance of Christianity to the widest possible range of political, social, educational, artistic, cultural and even scientific issues.

2. Congregations that can grow

Second, those congregations that have sufficient desire to grow seem to be able to do so. In itself this does not seem to be remarkable, but it is all too easy to forget that as recently as the 1960s and 1970s it seemed to be virtually impossible for any congregation to grow. In 1979, the MARC Europe census conducted among English churches resulted in a report which included the comment, 'some churches of every denomination are growing in every part of England'. That finding was newsworthy in 1979. The past fifteen years have seen the emergence of many growing churches to such an extent that church growth is no longer news. What is now at issue is not so much whether churches can grow; it is whether the members of a particular church are ready to make growth a sufficient priority that they are willing to make necessary changes in the life of their church.

3. New, large congregations

Third, there is evidence from many cities across Europe of the emergence of large congregations that have something of the character of celebration in their major worship services. Some of these congregations have grown from relatively small numbers of people to many hundreds over the past few years. A few now number thousands of people in their weekly congregations. Nearly all have good reason to believe that they will continue to grow strongly over the next few years. They stand in stark contrast to the large but empty buildings belonging to some of the historic denominations found all across Europe. These newer congregations share a number of common characteristics:

They stress spirituality. It may seem strange to single out this element. After all, don't all churches deal with spirituality? Surprisingly, many Christian congregations are very uncomfortable with the notion of spirituality if by that one means any kind of significant experiential encounter with God. Many churches, especially in the Reformed tradition, are much more inclined to engage in teaching and thus talk about God, rather than encourage their members to encounter God in ways other than cerebral comprehension.

In his seminal work on post-modernity, David Harvey highlights the differences between modernity and post-modernity using a list originally devised by another author. He points out that modernity and post-modernity contain a different emphasis in the way they approach the Trinity. Modernity tends to see God as God the Father while post-modernity makes a much stronger connection with God as the Holy Spirit.[5] A view of God which emphasises God as Holy Spirit helps to facilitate an experiential spirituality.

They practise innovative ministries. Past expressions of innovation are easy for us to identify. The work of a William Booth or a John Wesley has been vindicated by time, but the work of such men was not always viewed benignly. These newer, growing churches often invent highly innovative strategies to facilitate growth. One such church operates as a lay movement within the State church. Although their leaders are ordained ministers in Nonconformist churches they have laid down the privileges of such ordination in order to minister more effectively in their given situation.

They multiply leadership. A strong feature of the new and larger churches is that they take responsibility for their own training rather than sending their prospective leaders to a Bible or theological college. This emphasis on training is usually an extremely cost-effective means of training much larger numbers of leaders than could possibly be achieved by using external agencies. More critically, it allows the churches concerned to train their students in the specific skills that are needed to accomplish the programme that the congregation has adopted. Sending students to a training institution is usually much more 'hit and miss' in terms of ensuring that the skills which are learnt will feed back easily into the congregation that wants to use them.

The effect of this approach is to allow the congregation to reproduce the innovative culture that it has already developed. For this reason, most leadership appointments take place within the life of the congregation. Very few leaders will be recruited from entirely outside the congregation in the traditional manner of ministerial placement. Such congregations not only reproduce their own culture within the emerging leadership of the congregation, but also frequently export it in the form of church-planting strategies. Nearly all of these congregations have either already invested in church planting or are considering how they might do so.

They have crossed a culture barrier. It may only be one barrier that has been crossed. It could conceivably be more than one barrier. At the very least, all of these congregations have grown rapidly because they have been able to reach groups of people who would not normally think of becoming involved with the historic churches. It may be a very specific group, for example, young people, middle-class professionals with only a memory of church life but no actual experience, ethnic groups or even 'New Agers', but in some way a cultural nerve has been touched and explored by such congregations.

4. Divisions healed

Four, there is some evidence of a healing of the older liberal/ evangelical divide. This question was explored a little in Chapter 6 of this book. Theological as well as cultural developments have lessened the sharpness of the earlier divide, but the context for active engagement is worth noting. Until recently it was almost axiomatic that when evangelicals talked of mission they meant evangelism and when liberals talked of mission they meant everything except evangelism.

The recent Decade of Evangelism amongst Anglicans and to a lesser extent the Decade of Evangelisation amongst Catholics has helped to take this debate in a new direction. By focusing on evangelism it led some who stood outside an evangelical tradition to acknowledge that they did not know much about evangelism. Some were prepared to humbly suggest that they needed the insight of the evangelicals. At the same time, the more the Decade has progressed, the more evangelicals have come to realise that evangelism alone is not sufficient. The real issue is mission. Only an adequate framework will allow creative evangelism to emerge in the newly developing context of modernity becoming post-modernity. For some years, especially in the English context, there have been growing moves to encourage those of an evangelical and liberal churchmanship to work together in mission. These moves have been given a particular focus in relation to a number of key projects. In other words, these initiatives have not taken place as a theoretical construct ('wouldn't it be good if we could work together') but rather have been given a pragmatic urgency because of the need to work together if particular ends are to be achieved. Although it does not serve the purposes of this book to discuss such initiatives in detail, one such example would be the various local, as well as national, initiatives flowing from the Challenge 2000 project.

Building a missionary church

The initial realisation that Europe had become a mission field, documented so starkly by the French worker priests in the early 1940s, was slow to enter the consciousness of the ordinary church attender in Europe. In some ways the notion that Europe was somehow a Christian continent was maintained even more fondly by those who never attended a church other than for the traditional functions of christenings, weddings and funerals. It is only recently, more than fifty years after that initial work was published, that the implications of the reality are beginning to be taken seriously. The churches have been painfully slow to understand the extent of the task that needs to be undertaken.

The initial response to the situation was really a call to intensify all that had gone before. In other words, there were calls to be more effective in serving the community, for churches to hold 'a mission', to learn more about evangelism, sometimes even a plea for more clergy so that contact with non-churchgoers could be increased. Clergy started to be more aware of the evangelistic opportunities that such matters as the 'rites of passage' offered. Courses and programmes such as Evangelism Explosion and Church Growth began to appear. More than 25,000 church leaders in England and Wales alone attended the Bible Society's Church Growth courses in the period 1978 to 1993. The Billy Graham crusades of the 1980s offered a version of the same course under the title, 'Is my church worth joining?' Significant amounts of effort went into helping churches to grow and it is certainly possible to find churches that did grow as a result of good pastoral practice.

However, this intensification of effort has resulted largely in the more-effective gathering in of the fringe of church. Some very effective congregations succeeded in expanding their fringe as well as evangelising it. But such an approach to the problem of Europe as a mission field essentially sees evangelism and mission as 'bolt-on' extras. In other words they are things that one does in addition to the main task of being a pastoral and teaching community. Evangelism is viewed as the outreach arm that helps to add to the main body, but the main body is still essentially concerned with the maintenance of its own life.

During the 1980s there were some calls to help churches move from 'maintenance to mission'. But the content of such calls was never entirely clear. Often such calls really meant little more than the freeing of resource to allow more to be focused on the missionary task of the church. Less spent on the building, more spent on evangelism. There was very little attempt to see a fundamental change in the way in which the church operated.

In very recent years some much more fundamental thinking has taken place concerning the mission of the church in Europe. In part this new work has been undertaken by many who had been missionaries in other lands and who returned to Europe only to become much more acutely aware that what was now required in their homeland was precisely the missionary insight used to great effect on other mission fields. Many such returned missionaries have helped to challenge the church at a whole variety of levels to rethink its task in Europe radically. At a local church level, David Pytches has offered new models for church planting and church life. At a diocesan level, Pat Harris has brought many insights from his time as a missionary in South America to the task he faces. In the theological sphere, returned missionaries such as Lesslie Newbigin and Dan Beeby have helped the church to see the nature of the missionary task with greater clarity. Others besides these returned missionaries have prompted some significant reflection on the nature of mission in Europe.

A number of recent initiatives in England from widely different segments of the church have been formed and have gradually become aware of each other. Three of these serve as useful illustrations of a new and more fundamental approach to the task of mission. Canon Robert Warren has begun to reflect on the missionary church in his role as an officer for the Decade of Evangelism. It is significant that reflection on the Decade of Evangelism should have led Robert Warren in the direction of advocating the building of missionary congregations as compared with merely equipping congregations to engage in more effective evangelism. The evangelism that is needed, not only for this decade but for the next century, can only flow from a missionary church.

Second, Donald Elliot, in his role as Secretary to the Council for World Mission, has engaged in similar work. This work may well result in a practical initiative springing from a body which is part of the ecumenical structure of the English churches. The implication of Donald's work is that the relationship of evangelism to mission has been very clearly considered.

Third, the Evangelical Alliance has suggested a project aimed at producing 'mission-minded congregations'. Discussions on this project are still at an early stage and so it would be unhelpful to describe the proposals in too much detail. However, conversations with those involved in all three of these processes suggests that very similar conclusions and processes are taking place across very diverse strands of churchmanship. These three initiatives are by no means all of those which are currently being developed, but if it turns out that the Evangelical Alliance, the Church of England and the Council for World Mission are seeing their thinking converge, then we might be entitled to a substantial suspicion that God is at work!

Those who are beginning to talk of a missionary church in Britain have seen that the former distinction between home mission and foreign mission simply cannot and must not be maintained. Such a division led inevitably to the idea that real mission always took place overseas and that the contribution of the church in Europe to mission was to send money and personnel overseas. Home mission has frequently been seen as either the provision of clergy or as the training of churches in evangelism. When I finished training for the ministry my own denomination had a Home Missions Committee whose sole function was to pay and place clergy. The previous title for the Committee had been the General Evangelistic Committee. Its function had been exactly the same before its name changed, with a slightly stronger emphasis on an earlier pattern of providing itinerant evangelists. Home mission was not really proper mission but only the maintenance of churches on the home front.

The ending of such a distinction will possibly be even more challenging for the missionary societies whose current focus is an overseas one than for the various home mission structures. How will the older missionary societies be helped to train, finance and enable mission in Europe? Newer agencies from a broadly evangelical camp already transcend this distinction. Organisations such as Youth With A Mission and Campus Crusade for Christ have never had a division between home and foreign missions. Is it possible for the older missionary societies to learn something from these newer agencies?

Tasks for a missionary church

The term 'church' is normally used in two ways. It can refer to a local congregation or to some aspect of the wider universal church. When talking about creating a missionary church both of these understandings of the church must be considered. The next chapter looks in more detail at what a missionary congregation might look like. Before we examine the local manifestation of a missionary church it is important to arrive at some understanding of what we mean by a missionary church in the broader sense of that word. What should a missionary church in the West look like? Clearly it should be composed of many local congregations which are missionary in their life and nature. But what are the urgent tasks that face the corporate life of the church in the West? Two issues in particular stand out as primary tasks.

1. An effective apologetic

The task of apologetics does not constitute evangelism. Apologetics act as a precursor to the evangelistic task. Alister McGrath makes the helpful point that apologetics does not create faith.[6] No-one has ever been argued into the kingdom of God. The task of apologetics is not to force people into faith by a form of intellectual bullying but rather to remove misconceptions about the Christian faith; in McGrath's words to 'create an intellectual and imaginative climate favourable to faith'. That task is doubly important in the mission field of the West where the dominant intellectual tradition is not only unfavourable to the faith but has become almost deliberately hostile to the Christian faith. Good apologetics helps to build points of contact where an open consideration of the claims of faith becomes possible. There are at least three ingredients in the apologetic task for a missionary church in the West.

A critique of society. It will be necessary to tackle the 'high ground' of Western culture. Christianity is not arguing that it is just one helpful way of looking at life. It is making the seemingly outrageous claim that all of life can only be understood properly from the perspective of the life, death and resurrection of Jesus Christ. It is not enough merely to make such a claim, no matter how passionately

Christians may believe it. That claim must be argued for, its validity demonstrated. This task is essential precisely because so many have dismissed the content of the Christian message before they have ever taken it seriously. The implications of such an intellectual climate are very important for every aspect of Christian activity. For example, the Bible Societies in the West do their very best to make the Bible accessible both overseas and in their own lands. In many continents the problems are the purely practical matters of translation, publication and distribution. But in the West the problems are very different. The issue in most Western countries is not the availability of the Bible; everyone can afford to buy a Bible and they exist in many translations, sizes, formats and editions. The problem is much more the fact that the message of the Scripture has been discounted before a single page has been read.

Engaging with the intellectual and artistic current of a whole culture demands a very thorough examination of the foundational presuppositions of that culture. What does that culture believe about the way in which knowledge is formulated? What hopes and fears does that culture contain? What is the basis for such themes? What traditions are so deep rooted that they can hardly be questioned? What constitutes authority in a given culture?

It would be normal for a missionary travelling to another culture to consider these issues and it is not as difficult for the outsider to identify the answers to these questions as it is for those who have lived all their lives within such a tradition. This is partly why Islam has been able to develop a coherent and comprehensive critique of Western culture. Islamic scholarship draws on an intellectual tradition that is very distinct from that of the West. It is much more difficult for those who have been formed by a culture to identify and describe those assumptions. However, there are those scholars, such as Lesslie Newbigin, who are attempting to do just that. It is no coincidence that Newbigin has spent a significant part of his working life immersed in a totally different culture. As I have already commented, the work of missionaries who have either returned to the West or who have come to the West from other cultures will be vitally important in helping the Western church with this task.

Beyond critique. It is one thing to offer a creative critique of a society, it is quite another to suggest constructive alternatives. I recently heard one evangelical leader speak of the openness of European leaders to hear a Christian voice. His encounter with such leaders indicated a broad agreement with a Christian critique of Western society. However, the evangelical leader in question soon realised that when challenged to offer constructive alternatives, Christian answers are not nearly as well developed as the initial analysis of the problem. Nor is it enough to offer theoretical alternatives. The alternatives have to be lived and modelled in order to be demonstrated effectively. My book *The Faith of the Unbeliever* argues that Christians are not always as clear as they might be about the message that we proclaim. A good deal of work remains to be done in this area.[7]

Addressing objections. Those who are not yet ready to accept positive arguments for the Christian faith also have their own well-developed objections to the Christian faith. Again, in *The Faith of the Unbeliever* I suggest that the actual life of the institutional church and our advocacy of the authority of the Bible often represents a weakness in the face of a well-argued attack on Christianity.[8] There remains a great deal of work for the Christian community to do if it is to mount an effective apologetic which answers objections to the Christian faith.

Having said this, the growing recognition that the experiment of the Enlightenment has largely failed offers the Christian apologist an intriguing new context for debate. As David Harvey has pointed out, the target for the Christian apologist has shifted.[9] Twenty years ago Marxism and secular liberalism represented the major ideologies which resisted Christianity, but these have now lost their compelling power. Post-modernity is more open to a Christian critique if for no other reason than the fact that its debating method recognises the validity of the faith statement. Indeed, because Christianity has never recognised the all-sufficiency of reason alone and yet seeks to maintain that the revelation of God that comes in Jesus Christ is consistent with reason, it may yet help to steer post-modernity to more certain ground.

2. Strategic alliances

The liberal/evangelical divide that has so afflicted the church during the twentieth century tended to see cooperation between Christians in two very different ways. There has been a tendency for Christians in the 'ecumenical' camp to see co-operation in institutional and organic terms and for those in an evangelical tradition to look more towards the concept of the 'spiritual' unity of Christians at the level of a common commitment to Christ. Although this picture is an oversimplification of the situation, these broad differences of approach have nevertheless impacted patterns of Christian co-operation. In the area in which I live clergy meet in two very distinct fraternals. One is associated with the local Council of Churches and the other is an informal gathering of evangelical clergy from a more loosely defined area. The subjects that these fraternals discuss are significantly different from each other and the speakers that each group chooses are rarely, if ever, the same. I certainly know of other areas where this kind of divide is gradually being overcome but it remains a common pattern. It is rarely a hostile pattern but it is not a missionary pattern.

The point about both these groups (apart from their mutual isolation) is that the unconscious models they use for co-operation are not helpful. The institutional model is not sufficiently flexible while the informal approach rarely produces high levels of commitment to anything beyond meeting for the sake of fellowship. A missionary church needs to be able to develop models of co-operation which can best be described as campaigning models. As in the field of apologetics, Christians need to have a clearer idea of what they are for rather than what they are against. Christians often have a deep sense of unease about the apparent direction in which our culture seems to be moving but we have not been very precise in articulating the kinds of changes that we want to see in society. In part this is because Christians have seen themselves as defending a Christian heritage within society and therefore have often felt the need to oppose change. The positive advocacy of change has been more difficult for Christians to grasp.

There are some grounds for believing that the growing evangelical wing of the church is now moving in the direction of strategic or campaigning co-operation. In some ways, the Billy Graham crusades of the late 1940s and early 1950s, with his organisation's insistence on obtaining widespread endorsement across the denominational spectrum, served as an early model of what could be accomplished in terms of practical evangelism when churches worked together. This evangelical model of ecumenism has gradually grown, becoming increasingly diverse and strategic as time has passed by.

In Britain, evangelicals have co-operated in events such as Spring Harvest which now brings close to 100,000 evangelicals together for weeks of teaching, worship, preaching and inspiration. The March for Jesus organisation is now able to mobilise as many as 250,000 Christians in an activity on one single day. National prayer conventions attract as many as 15,000 people at a single event. The organisation Challenge 2000 seeks to mobilise evangelicals in a national church-planting strategy with the goal of planting as many as 20,000 new churches in Britain by the year 2000. Cross-denominational co-operation amongst evangelicals is increasingly evident in local initiatives as well as national events. In Peckham, London, a coalition of evangelical churches has been active in a local employment and training scheme that has been so successful that it has won plaudits from the national secular media. In the United Kingdom, in 1994 alone, three major nation-wide evangelistic initiatives, the JIM campaign, Minus to Plus and On Fire, were pioneered by evangelicals. Whatever the relative merits or otherwise of these particular initiatives the general impact has been to enable the life of local congregations to have much more effect than if they were acting in isolation. The days when evangelicals were divided, suspicious of others and of each other, are now almost a distant memory. These changes have taken place within the last fifty years, and although it is true that they apply much more extensively to English-speaking countries than in the West more generally, the same trend can be demonstrated across the Western world. Pan-evangelical confidence and action is evident as a growing feature of Western Christianity.

This growth of a broader evangelical co-operation is highly reminiscent of the growing strategic co-operation which took place at the beginning of the nineteenth century, flowing directly from the revival movement of the late eighteenth century and helping to foster the impact of revival throughout the nineteenth century. A number of authors have explored the extent to which Wilberforce and the other members of the so called 'Clapham Sect', were instrumental in welding together an effective evangelical strategy for changing the course of the nation.[10] The multi-faceted nature of this strategy, ranging from political lobbying to produce social change, through to organisations to promote social care, missionary work and even the production of Bibles, forms a remarkable picture. For Wilberforce, the vitally important insight was that evangelicals could only influence the course of the nation through united action. No matter how strong individual congregations might be, as long as evangelicals remained isolated from each other, or even worse, hostile to one another, their numerical strength yielded few benefits in terms of any wider impact. In the view of one author who did not approve of evangelical action:

~~At the close of the Napoleonic Wars, the organized activities of~~
missionary societies, tract societies, Sunday schools, and Bible societies, with the allied and competitive work of other groups, was subjecting the British population to an intellectual, emotional, and moral pressure such as Western civilization had not seen before.[11]

Pentecostal/Charismatic renewal

But is it realistic to imagine that evangelical Christianity, despite its current ascendancy, its strong local churches and increasingly united activity, could really produce a similar impact at the end of the twentieth century in the Western world? It could be argued that there has been no recent revival movement in Western lands equivalent to the revivals which provided the dynamism which powered evangelical activity in the nineteenth century. However, such a perspective overlooks the impact that the Pentecostal/Charismatic movement is beginning to have in a Western context. The early leaders of the Pentecostal movement all expressed the hope that this would be a movement which would renew the existing churches. The model of the holiness movement, that had remained inside the life of many denominations in Europe, was used as an example. Although these leaders often remained in their respective historic denominations all their lives, the movement which they fostered did not. Nowhere in the Western world has the classical Pentecostal movement become a dominant expression of Christianity in the way that it has become in some settings amongst the newer mission fields. In Britain, it would be relatively easy to dismiss the impact of the white-led Pentecostal churches which have a combined membership of around 100,000.

However, this assessment overlooks the growing impact of 'Pentecost outside of Pentecost'. The spread of a Pentecostal spirituality, first in the historic churches through the charismatic movement, second in the House Church movement (now called the New Churches), more recently in the Vineyard movement and even more recently through the so-called 'Toronto blessing', has huge implications for mission. The diversity of this spirituality, illustrated by what some have called the various waves of this expression of Christianity, has at times seemed more important than its essential underlying unity. As each new wave, or expression, has arrived, there has often been tension with some of those in the preceding wave or waves. For example, the Pentecostal denominations were initially very hostile to the arrival of the Charismatic movement in the historic churches. The leaders of the Charismatic movement were initially aggrieved by the development of the House Churches. Some House Church leaders were initially somewhat suspicious of the development of Wimber's influence in the context of the Vineyard churches.

Other more complex and competitive elements within these streams could also be described. But the most significant development of recent years has not been the increasing diversity, though that remains, so much as the growing interrelation and co-operation between these complementary streams of Pentecostal spirituality. The impact of a high degree of co-operation between the various streams of this common spirituality has the potential to provide an equivalent force to that which flowed from earlier revival movements. Indeed, one consequence of such co-operation might even be to help foster the conditions for the outbreak of similar revivals.

The importance of this growing Pentecostal stream can be seen in at least four key areas. First, it has helped to change theological thinking at a popular level. The idea of spiritual gifts is now commonplace in church life even if the theological categories which are used to describe them vary. I would want to argue that such a change in theological emphasis has had its impact on the way in which Christians think about the nature of the church, especially with regard to its ministry and the laity. The actual experience of spiritual gifts given to every member of the body of Christ has the practical effect of demonstrating the priesthood of all believers.

Second, it has brought renewed confidence to a church in the West which has often felt defeated and powerless. The sheer vitality of worship that has flowed from Pentecostal spirituality is reflected in the enormous flowering of hymnody which has emanated from this segment of the church. That vitality has brought encouragement and a renewal of vigour for many Christians. Creative and innovative approaches to mission and evangelism tend to flow from churches which display confidence and vitality.

Third, it has brought a common language of spirituality, experience and expectation. This commonalty has allowed some surprising barriers to be transcended. Christians that have not been in active co-operation with others for many years have found that a common experience of the Spirit produces a level of understanding that often brings greater unity between those with a common charismatic experience in different denominations than between those who do not share such an experience but belong to the same denomination. Increasingly, the leadership of many significant local churches and of many denominations do share in such a spirituality.

Fourth, the commonalty of experience has led to the development of deep friendships amongst Christian leaders across all previous boundaries. A closer look at the growing success of many pan-evangelical alliances reveals that many of the leaders not only share a common Pentecostal or Charismatic experience but also they are close friends. The suspicions of earlier years are being overcome.

The development of these connections within the various Pentecostal streams can all too easily be taken for granted as if they were simply inevitable, but they are certainly not. In fact, there is one stream within the broader Pentecostal family which has been very difficult to absorb, namely the so called 'Health and Wealth' teaching frequently associated with Kenneth Hagin and others. This particular stream has been largely insignificant within Britain and in any case has tended to moderate its teaching in recent years. However, in some European countries, notably in Scandinavia, this particular stream has made a greater relative impact. The lack of integration of this stream within the broader family of Pentecostal spirituality has severely impaired the development of partnership in these countries. The consequences of a lack of unity across Pentecostal streams in some lands serves to underline the achievements that have taken place where such co-operation is well advanced.

To date, most of this co-operation has been aimed at evangelism or church planting. Despite early indications that evangelicals are becoming increasingly involved in social issues, the extent to which strategic campaigning alliances are being used to mobilise large sections of the church to produce changes in society are so far rather limited. In other words, the attempt of Wilberforce and his friends to exert 'intellectual, emotional, and moral pressure such as Western civilization had not seen before' has yet to be repeated.

Notes

1. Jonathan Sacks, *The Persistence of Faith*, p. 1.
2. John Drane, *Evangelism for a New Age*, p. 14.
3. *Ibid.*, p. 18.

4. *Ibid.*, p. 14.
5. David Harvey, *The Condition of Postmodernity*, p. 41.
6. Alister McGrath, *Bridge Building*, p. 81.
7. Martin Robinson, *The Faith of the Unbeliever*, pp. 180ff.
8. *Ibid.*, pp. 185ff.
9. David Harvey, *op. cit.*, p. 41.
10. Charles Foster, *An Errand of Mercy*, pp. 82ff.
11. *Ibid.*, p. 99.

CHAPTER TEN

THE ELEMENTS OF A MISSIONARY CONGREGATION

It is all very well to talk about mission in the West as if it was the unique concern of a few specialists. But much more will be needed if the whole church is to become missionary in its life and concern in the context of the Western world. Mission is no longer what we send money to in order that others might go and engage in mission elsewhere. Mission is now all around us. Ourselves, our local church; we are the ones who are called to be missionaries just where we are. Newbigin speaks of 'the congregation as the hermeneutic of the gospel'.[1] Bearing that in mind, what will a local missionary congregation actually look like, or even more particularly, what will it do?

In some respects, the local congregation which has a missionary orientation looks no different from any other congregation. Praise and worship of God still stand at the centre of the life of any congregation. The very act of worship declares and proclaims the truth to which the Christian community bears witness. The pastoral task goes on — in some respects it becomes even more important as needy people enter the life of the church. The teaching task continues — the business of teaching the fundamentals of the faith becomes more urgent in a missionary situation, but it is essentially the same task that the church has always had. However, there are some tasks which the missionary church has to engage in which previously may have stood at the fringes of the life of the church. These tasks need to become central in the awareness of local missionary congregations.

Over the last few years I have suggested to a number of groups what a missionary congregation might look like. From time to time I have been pleased to learn after the event that some of those who have been present have been missionaries in various parts of the world. It has been gratifying to learn that the picture that I have described is one with which they are familiar. This is an important issue. A missionary congregation in one part of the world is not essentially different in character from one in another part of the world. The character of a missionary church should be universal in nature even if the precise application of the principles varies.

In his book *Building Missionary Congregations* Robert Warren[2] reflects on the need for the deliberate intent to build missionary congregations in the West. By this he does not mean beginning entirely new congregations (although this is not excluded) so much as helping existing churches to make the transition from maintenance to mission. In his appendix he lists what he calls 'the marks of a missionary congregation'.[3] In other words, what a missionary congregation would do. A number of other thinkers and writers have produced other such lists. As I read these various lists, I rarely find myself thinking, 'a missionary congregation would not do that'. In other words, part of our difficulty in arriving at a description of a missionary congregation is that we can set the church, or indeed ourselves, an impossible agenda. A missionary congregation cannot do everything and yet there is very little that is ruled out!

With that difficulty in mind, I have tried to produce an agenda for a missionary congregation which is neither exhaustive nor exhausting. In suggesting the following elements for a missionary congregation I have tried to produce an irreducible minimum rather than an inclusive maximum — to indicate those elements without which a congregation can scarcely be a missionary body at all.

1. Employing missionary strategies

Establishing the church

When facing a missionary challenge the first reaction of Christians may not be to establish the church so much as to simply evangelise. The recent opening of the countries of the former Soviet Union enabled many Christian groups (and others) to enter from the West. Two responses were quickly in evidence: the desire to offer aid and the intention to evangelise. Many evangelists adopted familiar Western forms, particularly that of the crusade meeting. The first to engage in this practice were amazed to discover that nearly everyone in the crowds that came responded to the invitation to accept Christ, whether by raising a hand or by coming forward at the time of the appeal. It did not take too long to discover that these commitments often had no meaning (beyond their obvious value in raising funds in the West). Those present had no real way of understanding what such a response meant. Some were merely trying to be polite, others responded at every meeting they attended. Those who intended to stay and work in these areas soon realised that the establishing of local congregations was of the utmost importance if the work of evangelism was to go forward.

In the West, where many congregations already exist, those who wish to see existing congregations become missionary in their character and so move from mainte-nance to mission soon see that it is not an easy task. Many who belong to congregations of long-standing often see those congregations in terms of maintaining a tradition — a memory of how things have been, even a family or cultural inheritance — before agreeing that mission forms the main agenda of the church. Strengthening the church for survival so that these inherited and often very local traditions are maintained is often the single priority. The kind of growth that brings traumatic change is not welcomed. In such situations it can take a very long time to move from maintenance to mission.

Some leaders are not prepared to wait for such change to take place and so look to church planting to produce a new congregation that has a strong mission agenda built into its foundations. If change is to come in an existing situation it will often be because the same principles that are applied in a church-planting situation are utilised in order to replant the existing congregation. Robert Warren makes the helpful point that making the transition from maintenance to mission does not simply mean becoming more active. He suggests that some congregations have moved from a 'passive pastoral mode' to an 'activist pastoral mode',[4] but that shift should not be confused with becoming a missionary congregation. The challenge is to shift the entire focus of the congregation from pastoring to mission.

Robert Warren describes the level of change that is required as a conscious 'opting for change'.[5] Producing change of that degree is sufficiently complex to require particular skills, all the more so because in a culture where rapid change is impacting so many areas of life that the term 'Future Shock' has been coined to describe the phenomenon, the church is often looked to as the place which insulates its members from change. The change process both deserves and requires more attention than this chapter or indeed this book can properly afford. Those who wish to encourage a transition to a missionary congregation must be properly equipped to facilitate significant change.

Dealing with culture

Whether a church is newly planted or whether it is an older congregation that has undergone enough change to make mission a priority, it will be necessary for a missionary congregation to understand the culture of those that it seeks to reach with the gospel message. There is a widespread assumption that those who have been brought up in the West already understand the culture in which they are set. While some gifted leaders have an intuitive grasp of the culture around them, they are few and far between. Even when they do exist their approach can often be misunderstood by their fellow Christians in the wider Christian world. They can be sure that their intuitive grasp of the surrounding world, together with the strategies they follow as a consequence, will attract widespread criticism from other Christians. One Christian leader in Britain who has successfully utilised the media, particularly television, for the gospel, has spoken of his pain when critical letters from Christians arrive at the television station. The secular staff members at the station are even more surprised at such a response. 'Aren't they supposed to be on your side?' they comment.

The task of helping those other than intuitive evangelists to understand secular and post-secular Western people is only just beginning. It will be a long road to travel. The landscape of unbelief is a complex terrain. Those who call themselves unbelievers do not believe nothing at all. On the contrary, they believe a great deal and it is the content of those beliefs rather than the absence of belief that forms the first barrier to communication for a missionary church.[6]

It would seem likely that those who have recently become Christians from an unchurched background would be best equipped to communicate with those who are still unchurched. Certainly such individuals often do have some advantages. Beyond the first wild excesses of trying to

convert everyone, they will still know and use the language
of unbelievers. They may even be considered 'normal'
people who can be trusted with inquiries from some who
are in spiritual pain. But it is still the case that even those
who have been converted from such a background are often
puzzled by their own former resistance to faith and by the
continued hardness of those family and friends who share
their former unbelief. They may know how to talk in order
to be understood and accepted by unchurched people, but
the question of why people should be so seemingly unrec-
eptive and of how to overcome such barriers is often just as
perplexing to such new believers as it is to others who have
grown up within the nurture of the church.

The task of understanding Western culture needs to take
place at two levels. The West has lived with the basic
ingredients of secularism for hundreds of years. Understanding why it has become so hostile to the Christian faith in
recent times is an important task. Just as urgent is the task of
unravelling even newer developments in our culture. The
'cracks in modernity' to which I have already referred
need to be recognised so that Christianity can enter the
public debate on the future of our culture. This 'high' level
of encounter with our culture is so demanding that few
congregations will contain those who are engaged in such a
scholarly task. Fortunately there are a few who are beginning
this process. They need to be owned by the whole church.
They are certainly a gift to every local congregation because
their thoughts are accessible through books, conferences and
wider debate. The task of the local congregation is not
necessarily to produce such rare individuals so much as to
interpret the import of what they are saying.

The second level is that of taking these insights and seeing
how they might be incorporated into the activity of the local
church. For example, some research is indicating that the
heart cry of secular people is to find ways of establishing
meaningful and satisfying relationships. This heart cry is

often, though not always, focused on establishing a basis for good family life. At first sight this might seem to be something of a paradox. The rapid and all too frequent breakdown of marriages, the pressures on family life, the reluctance of many to enter committed relationships of any kind would seem to suggest that relationships are the last thing to interest anyone in the West. Yet every available piece of research that we have suggests that the breakdown of relationships is both a puzzle and a source of despair for many in the West. It is not that people care nothing for relationships, it is more that they have very little knowledge of how to make them work. Christians do not have all the answers in this area. Christians live in the same secular world that non-Christians inhabit and are subject to the same pressures, but we do have access to some important resources in tackling this problem both for ourselves and for others.

Developing the church

Churches do not simply grow of their own accord. Even apart from the action of God, a great deal of hard work in terms of developing appropriate structures which can facilitate growth often accompanies the growth of any congregation. Leaders have a responsibility to organise the life of the church. The largest church in the world, the Full Gospel Church in Seoul, Korea is a highly organised and disciplined organisation. Such structures are not the whole story of the church by any means but they are part of it. Once again, there are those gifted individuals who just know what to do though they have never learned in any formal way how to develop the church. Most leaders can learn to develop these skills in the same way that a naturally gifted musician can learn from others how to enhance their musical gift.

Relatively simple insights can serve to unlock the growth potential of many churches. For example, the issue of what leadership style is appropriate in relation to the particular size of a congregation can allow a leader to overcome potential barriers to growth. To learn when and how to delegate is vital in releasing and mobilising the gifts of others. Knowing how to build teams so that one or two individuals do not dominate will help congregations to develop their full potential.

2. Evangelism

The Anglican church in England gave an important lead to other churches at the end of the 1980s by calling for a Decade of Evangelism. Not long after that call, the Roman Catholic church began talking about a Decade of Evangelisation. The different terms caused some initial confusion in Britain. What term should be used? Early reactions tended to reflect the view that this was only a matter of semantics and therefore it did not matter what word was used. More careful reflection reveals that there is a good deal of difference between these two concepts. 'Evangelisation' describes the task of evangelising a whole culture. It is a way of acknowledging that there has been a divorce between the culture of the West and the Christian faith that nurtured and shaped so much of the West's heritage. Even the former pre-Christian glories of Rome and Greece were largely, if not entirely mediated to the West through the church. The notion of evangelisation helps the church to see that it is not just the case that individuals need to embrace faith in Christ, the whole of society needs to be informed by the teachings of Christ. The media, education, politics, economics, law, family and much more need to be transformed by the message of the gospel.

Evangelism refers more particularly to the taking of the gospel message to individuals. It is very hard for local congregations to engage in the task of evangelisation since it is such a large task. But it is important for the local church to undertake the evangelistic task with the broader perspective of evangelisation in mind. It is possible, indeed likely, that some congregations will be able to make a contribution to the task of the re-evangelisation of the West, even though on a day-to-day basis, the work of evangelism is a more immediate concern. What aspects of evangelism should occupy the attention of a missionary church?

Witness

The New Testament word for witness, *martur*, gave rise to the modern English word 'martyr'. So many of the early Christians gave witness and were killed for doing so that the two words became strongly associated with each other. Bearing witness can still be an uncomfortable matter even though few of us in the West expect to become martyrs as a result. But what does bearing witness really mean? Both living and speaking are inseparable parts of the call of a witness. Clearly our words will have little meaning unless they are matched by a lifestyle which by itself bears witness to the commitment we have made. There are some Christians who believe that a silent witness of works is sufficient, but in a world where so few understand much about the Christian faith, such an approach is at the best very optimistic. Would you be able to guess at the beliefs of a Zoroastrian by the way he or she lived if there was never any conversation on the matter?

Witnesses are called to give an account of their faith; to say what becoming or simply being a Christian means to them. This is not the same thing as giving a convincing survey of the claims of Christ, or explaining the intricacies of one or other of the theories of the atonement. It simply means telling your story. Most people can be encouraged to tell their story and in the process to re-examine and deepen that same story.

Being a witness might also result in the issuing of an

invitation. When speaking to different groups both in Britain and elsewhere, I always enjoy asking someone how they became a Christian. I have been surprised at how many people have pointed to a rather simple invitation to attend an event or even a regular worship service. These invitations were not issued by expert evangelists but by very ordinary Christians naturally exhibiting their desire to bear witness.

Equipping the evangelists

Although it is the call of every Christian to be a witness, not every Christian is an evangelist. It is sometimes suggested by church growth writers such as Peter Wagner that on average some 10 per cent of Christians are gifted as evangelists. Whether such a statement is authentic or not does not really matter to a local congregation, since Wagner is speaking of an average across the whole church. In practice, local congregations may find that their members contain a higher or lower average than this. What matters is not the existence of some hypothetical average so much as discovering who are evangelists, regardless of their actual number.

How can we recognise potential evangelists in our midst? Two qualities tend to be important. Evangelists are natural communicators. They are able to present the truth of the Christian message in forms and images that make sense to those around them. Second, they often have a natural curiosity about people, about their story, their situation and what drives them. Strangely, not every evangelist is as good at making small talk as they are at being able to turn the conversation to the basic issues of the gospel. I have met evangelists who are highly driven to seek out those who have a desire to explore spiritual issues but who are not nearly as good at maintaining relationships outside of these central concerns. This latter is not a requirement for an evangelist. Some who are gifted as evangelists do enjoy being around people, no matter what the issue might be, but we should not assume that everyone who is good with people is also gifted as an evangelist. Some who are good with people might be gifted more as pastors than evangelists.

But whatever the precise makeup of an evangelist, such people do exist in most congregations. Their natural giftedness can be enhanced by specific training. A knowledge of the most common objections to faith and of how to meet those objections helps. Familiarity with illustrations of what the gospel means in terms of examples from everyday life assists the communication process. Evangelists can be taught to understand something of the normal stages which mark a spiritual journey.[7] They can be trained in how to help someone's spiritual journey. It is essential that enough leaders in a congregation model evangelism by engaging in the evangelistic task themselves. Their regular involvement in evangelism results in the introduction of stories and illustrations in sermons and other regular contact with the members of the congregation. Such frequent communication helps to build a local church culture whereby evangelism becomes a normal and familiar part of a congregation's expectation. Leaders who model evangelism themselves create an environment which fosters the emergence of the natural evangelists in the congregation.

Evangelistic strategy

Even though evangelism depends crucially on the existence of many personal relationships with those outside the Christian community, good evangelistic strategies also play a part in generating such relationships. Many local congregations already have an implicit conviction about how evangelism takes place. Local traditions strongly suggest normative evangelistic strategies. What matters is not the precise formulation of these strategies so much as whether the strategies actually work. It is very easy for congregations to remain highly committed to strategies that have ceased to work. Very frequently a particular individual will see their own experience of becoming a Christian as the normal means by which all become Christians.

~~Some years ago I learned the practice of door-to-door~~ visitation as an evangelistic method. The person who taught me was highly motivated in such calling. After one fruitless evening visiting homes in a large complex of apartments I was ready to give up, but my instructor was keen to keep calling. I wanted to know what it was that fired his enthusiasm. He told me that he used to live in one of these apartments and that one night someone called on his home to tell him about Christ. That was the start of his journey to find faith. It provided powerful motivation for his conviction that this was an effective strategy.

This was a commendable attribute but there was also the possibility that his own experience prevented him from considering whether other strategies might be more effective. Evaluating the effectiveness of particular approaches to the evangelistic task is essential in continuing to review the methods used by a congregation. The heart of any good method lies in its ability to generate and develop relationships with unchurched people. A congregation might well be active in the task of witnessing and effective at identifying and training their natural evangelists but these developments must be accompanied by good evangelistic strategies if they are to bear real fruit. John Clarke, an Anglican clergyman, has recently written a book based on detailed research entitled *Evangelism that Really Works*.[8] His survey and case studies represent an extremely useful aid to choosing an evangelistic strategy.

3. Making disciples

What is a disciple? The word literally means one who follows a teacher or instructor. The idea of following includes much more than merely learning in a classroom or lecture situation. The disciples of Jesus were learning as much, if not more, from what he did, his character, his example and relationships with others, as they did from any formal teaching that he gave. The element of mentoring to enable them to 'do these things and greater than these things' was powerfully present. The sending out of the disciples to minister on their own represented a key ingredient in the learning process. They not only discovered who Jesus was, they also found out who they were. The failure of Peter in his denial of the Christ and his subsequent commissioning was as important as any other lesson he might have learnt. This was character formation at the coal-face.

The Great Commission in Matthew 28 includes the injunction to go and make disciples of all nations. Throughout the period of Christendom such a command made little sense. In the nations of Christendom, all were baptised, all were believers in the sense that there were no other options seriously available. To be a Christian was to be civilised, to be a Christian was to be human. The values of Christianity were mediated through the culture as much as, if not more than, through the local church. The local church did not act as a guardian of the faith, rather it was required to conform to the broader norms of a Christian society.

The development of modernity has produced a situation where the majority values of society are no longer anchored to the Christian faith. Western culture no longer mediates the values of Christian faith. If new converts are to understand what it means to be taught a Christian lifestyle, it will be because the Christian community transmits it to them. Failure to do this will mean that new converts will simply bring the values of the surrounding culture into the church. But what does it mean to help a new believer become a fully functioning disciple?

Bible knowledge

Traditionally, the church in the West during this present century has taken a rather cerebral approach to faith and discipleship. Therefore, the tendency has been to equate discipleship with Bible reading, Bible knowledge and Christian doctrine. That kind of knowledge certainly has an important place in the discipleship process. However, it is not sufficient by itself. Three other areas are critically important and need to run alongside the development of a good knowledge of the Bible.

Developing relationships

New converts need to learn how to relate to others in the church. This might sound both obvious and simple but it is neither. The radical individualism of the secular West causes those who imbibe such a culture to have enormous problems with such matters as commitment and the building of long-term relationships. It doesn't take much imagination to consider what takes place in a local church when strong commitment in relationships is absent. Division, upset, unhappiness, rumour, refusal to work with others followed by an all-too-easy departure for another church. That familiar process has produced many spiritual wanderers who have a tendency to move from church to church, never really becoming committed in any situation before finally dropping out of church completely.

How can one help people steeped in radical individualism to take relationships more seriously? The key to this process lies in helping such converts to tell each other the truth. This is a potentially dangerous area. I am not talking about producing a series of painful confrontations as the Christian norm. It is much more a matter of finding ways to deal with issues on a face-to-face basis rather than suppressing these matters, or even worse, telling everyone else how one feels about others in the church. Building a foundation of grace, love and acceptance is essential. Leaders need to model this acceptance and then they need to encourage others who have been so loved to extend that acceptance to others. The small-group context is almost certainly the most helpful means of exploring what it means to be committed to one another in relationships. The small-group leader will be greatly helped if they can point to the example of close long-term relationships within the leadership team. A breakdown of relationships amongst leaders causes members to be very cautious concerning the extent of their own commitment.

Personal encounter with God

New converts need to be taught how to have their own relationships with God rather than depending on the guidance and experiences of others. There is no substitute for experience in this area. Practical approaches in prayer, patient listening, trial and error to learn to recognise how God speaks to us; these are all part of the process of spiritual development. In past days many have assumed that prayer and spiritual matters are so private that they may not be discused with others. The outcome of this situation can all too easily become one in which no prayer and no spiritual development take place. Practical encounter in the ministry leads one to discover that all too many adults are still praying in the forms that they learned as a child or in the first few days or weeks of their conversion. The difficult questions of the spiritual life also need to be tackled. Why do I find it hard to pray? What happens when God seems far away? How should I respond to depression? What about the growing awareness of a dark side to my personality? The growing popularity of retreats and of pilgrimage, suggests that the experiential aspect of spirituality is beginning to be reawakened in the Western church.

Gifts and ministry

Discipleship is not complete until each individual has discovered their unique giftedness and is exercising that gift in a ministry of some kind. One very fundamental mistake still made by many leaders surrounds the notion that it is the leader's task to motivate others. In truth, motivation is an internal mechanism. The key to motivation does not lie in responding to someone else's vision but in that unique combination of personal giftedness and personal passion which can awaken internal motivation. It is certainly true that a person might be sufficiently inspired by the vision presented by someone else to be motivated to contribute something towards that vision. But what they will want to contribute will be drawn from the area of their giftedness and passion and not by offering something that they cannot do at all. (I have met some who are so unaware of what their gifts actually are that they do want to contribute what they are not good at, but there is always considerable resistance from others in such a case.)

What do I mean by personal giftedness and personal passion? Let me give you an example. In my own case, I am highly motivated to begin new projects. I tend to see potential in certain areas and I am made in such a way that I will always want to explore the potential of a new situation. It excites me to do so. I also have a number of gifts which enable me to explore and develop new areas. Therefore, it is very likely that I will be motivated by a project which involves something new or different and in which the potential can be extracted with a visible end result in view. For example, writing a book could be viewed as a project which extracts potential from a core idea and is structured as a project with a very visible and practical outcome. This pattern is sufficiently embedded in me that I will tend to see potential and be somewhat motivated almost no matter what area of life is involved. But in practice, my motivation is further honed by a strong desire, or passion, to see individuals become Christians and strong churches emerge. That passion acts as a powerful filter to direct the gifts and motivational patterns of my life.

A good discipleship process works with people to help them discover the areas of their giftedness, to allow them to understand what motivates them and to see those areas integrated in a God-given vision for service. It is very important to either locate or create very specific avenues of service in order to employ gifts once they have been discovered. It will hardly be necessary to motivate people who have made these discoveries. The difficulty will rather be to find enough avenues of service in which to express such gifts. The skill of leadership lies in managing and directing the creativity of the members of the congregation towards agreed goals and objectives.

4. Effective apologetics

The previous chapter noted that at one level the task of apologetics is one for the whole church. The local congregation cannot be expected to produce its own apologists but it is possible to become acquainted with the work of those who are gifted in this area and then to seek to communicate those insights both to Christians in the congregation and to those who have an interest in the Christian faith. The faith needs to be both explained and advocated at a local level.

Explaining the faith

The traditional role of apologetics is to explain the major claims of the Christian faith in such a way that those claims are seen as understandable and reasonable. That task is not inconsiderable. The Christian apologist in the twentieth-century West begins with two very different problems in view. First, unlike earlier years, very little can be assumed about a person's knowledge of the Christian faith or of the Bible. Even in the much more favourable climate of the United States, where a recent poll suggests that 42 per cent of the population hold the Bible to be literally true, and only 11 per cent regard it as essentially a collection of untrue fables, only 50 per cent of adults could even name one of the four gospels. The position in other Western countries is even more difficult. The apologist must therefore begin by giving some outline of the content of the Christian faith.

The second problem is to demonstrate the essential reasonableness of the faith to an audience which is unfamiliar with the language of faith. Finding appropriate language to express Christian truth is a continual quest. The ideas and images which are necessary to explain Christian concepts to those outside the Christian faith change as popular culture changes. Stories, illustrations, and examples from everyday life are needed in order to communicate the message effectively.

Apart from these two more recent problems, the traditional task of apologetics involves finding points of contact from which to begin dialogue, and then overcoming the obstacles or barriers to faith that are frequently raised by those with doubts. Until relatively recently Christian apologetics have tended to centre on what we might call issues of truth. For example, 'Is it true that Jesus was raised from the dead?' or 'Is the Bible true?' The supposition that lies behind such an approach suggests that if the truth of these claims can be demonstrated then the barriers to faith will largely have been overcome. However, recent changes in Western culture have rendered this approach rather more obsolete. Those who are involved in dialogue with unbelievers report that questions of truth have been supplanted in the minds of many by a different concern. In the emerging and increasingly post-secular culture of the West, the question of whether something works seems to be more important than whether it is true in a propositional sense. The culture of modernity seemed to suggest that if something was true then it would, by definition, work. More recently that process seems to have been reversed so that increasingly there is a tendency to believe that if something works then it is probably true. Viewed from a Christian perspective, both of these starting points have their difficulties. But whatever the problems, the apologist cannot choose the starting point, he must shape his arguments around the starting point of those who are being addressed.

The increasing distance of many in the West from any active knowledge of the Christian faith inevitably means that the starting point for many is not only different in terms of the underlying approach ('Is it true?' as compared with 'Does it work?'), there is also a huge difference in terms of the issues that can be discussed. For example, even when I began my ministry twenty years ago, the starting point for talking with those outside of the church about matters of belief tended to move very quickly to the more central questions of Christian faith: 'What was the significance of the death of Jesus?' or 'How reliable is the text of the Bible?' or even, 'What does it mean to be a follower of Jesus?' These were all familiar religious questions. But today, it is almost impossible to move directly to these questions. The starting point is much more likely to be a very general religious question with very little immediate connection to matters of Christian doctrine. The questions, 'Does life have any meaning?' or 'What is the essential nature of man?', are often touched upon before coming to the more familiar Christian issues which once arose more quickly.

Advocating the faith

Both the tasks already discussed are significant and demanding, but they might also be described as in some sense, defending the faith. A missionary situation offers the opportunity to develop the task of apologetics in the direction of giving positive reasons for the place of Christian belief in everyday life. In other words, to advocate the faith. Where might such a direction lead? Those who are Christians and who are involved with areas of creativity have increasingly begun to speak about the way in which Christian belief helps to develop further creativity. Two examples from very different fields might help to illustrate this process.

Those involved in the world of art have increasingly commented on the extent to which a belief in the transcendent helps to release creative thought from the confines of an horizon which is restricted by an overconcern for the merely material world. It is not a coincidence that some of the greatest art throughout history has a strongly religious dimension. This is not to argue that only Christians can be great artists so much as to speak for the place of the religious and Christian contribution to the creative process in art. Christians also have an important contribution to make in the world of business, not least in understanding how individuals contribute to the creative process in organisational life. The Christian view of people as uniquely created and gifted individuals offers a much richer vein to explore than the idea that people can be viewed primarily as economic units.

Moving from a sound defence to creative attack by positively advocating the merits of a Christian world-view in almost every area of life helps the church to become an attractive missionary movement. In the future it will not just be a matter of helping Christians in local congregations to know why they believe but also helping them to know how Christian faith positively contributes to everyday life. There is much work to do in this field.

5. Strengthening spirituality

In more recent times, there has been a tendency in the Western church to identify spirituality with an entirely reflective tradition. At its most extreme, this tendency views mission as active — as advance, and spirituality as passive — as retreat. The connection between mission and spirituality is not always well understood. Historically, the relationship has been well established. The influence of Catholic writers on spirituality, such as Ignatius Loyola, on figures like John Wesley is also well established. The revival movements of the eighteenth and nineteenth centuries fused a deep concern for the spiritual life with a passionate concern for proclamation. That combination was not unknown to Loyola, nor was it to those who sought to raise the question of mission in the modern era. Three aspects of spirituality are important for the missionary church.

Facing the dark side

The development of the spiritual life inevitably raises many profound issues concerning such matters as motivation, ambition, personal sin, and flawed character as well as encountering acceptance, forgiveness, direction and personal integration. The desire to experience healing and wholeness is strongly present in the spiritual quest. The ecstatic and sometimes mystical experience of the overwhelming love of God (giving rise on occasion to holy laughter) can also be accompanied by an experience of plunging into the depths of despair when facing the unacceptable, the unknown, the unbearable dark side of our personality. Learning to embrace our dark side, in the way that God already has, is part of the growing process in the spiritual life. The alternative is to continue to condemn ourselves, masking that condemnation by passing judgement on others — the life of legalism.

Personal ethics

Part of discipleship involves what is often called 'steward-ship' — a set of decisions about wealth and other resources which helps the believer to reflect their belief system in their lifestyle. That personal commitment to a particular lifestyle needs to be undergirded by a spirituality which encounters God in the world in which we live and work. For example, Mother Theresa's decision to work with the destitute and dying was not simply formed out of a Christian approach to stewardship. Certainly stewardship is involved but such a commitment flows first and foremost from the conviction that God is to be found in the midst of suffering. It is both a response to an experience of God's love and a desire to find him in every corner of the creation that stands behind the walk of the disciple.

Commitment to society

The mark of holiness in the mainstream of Christian tradition is to seek for the transformation of society. That concern might be expressed through a quiet life of prayer or it may be reflected in a vigorous programme of social action. But whatever the process, the principle remains the same — Christians are called to care for God's world and for those who are in it. Much has been written and said about Chris-tianity's 'bias towards the poor' — meaning that Christians are called to offer practical assistance to the downtrodden, the impoverished, the sick and the needy. The gospel stands in opposition to structures and acts of injustice which perpe-tuate the misery of the poor. Christian mission inevitably includes a practical agenda for change.

These are some of the tasks at least that the missionary congregation is called to consider. It will not be possible for every congregation to engage in every aspect of mission. Some have particular calls and their life needs to reflect that fact. But taken together, the life of local congregations, engaged in mission, will take account of the agenda for mission that God brings before his whole church.

Notes

1. Lesslie Newbigin, *The Gospel in a Pluralist Society*, pp. 222ff.
2. See Chapter 9, p. 186.
3. The list in Robert Warren's book, *Building Missionary Congregations*, pp. 52ff., is as follows:
    Celebration
    Whole Life Christianity
    Simplicity
    Community
    Empowering
    Doing things differently
    Engaged
    Distinctive
    Still
4. *Ibid.*, p. 16.
5. *Ibid.*, p. 33.
6. For a detailed account of what 'unbelievers' believe, see Martin Robinson, *The Faith of the Unbeliever*.
7. The Engels scale used in church growth represents a useful tool for evaluating someone's journey towards faith. See Roy Pointer, *How Do Churches Grow?*, p. 165.
8. John Clarke, *Evangelism That Really Works*.

CHAPTER ELEVEN

WINNING THE WEST

The very title of this book, echoed as it is by the title of this chapter, suggests a key difficulty for the church in the area of mission. Are we right to talk of 'winning' anything? Does a concern for mission lead inevitably to making a choice between a crude Christian triumphalism or a form of Christian service that never seeks to reform society at its root? The issue of power in mission cannot be avoided.

The question of how Christians view power stands at the very heart of the Christian message in the form of a perplexing paradox. On the one hand Jesus challenged the powers of this world and was killed by them for doing so, but on the other, the weapons that he chose — willing self-surrender and a refusal to defend himself, spelled the end of those same powers. The victory of the powers only revealed their final weakness. The weakness of Jesus allowed the real power of God to be made known. We are familiar with this message and yet its meaning is never easily grasped. As Walter Wink writes:

> How could this defeat issue in such a victory? The Powers were as powerful the day after the crucifixion as the day before. Nothing had visibly changed. And yet everything had changed. For now the powers were forced to 'listen for the silent step of the dead man's invisible feet' and to contend with a spirit that 'walks through walls'.[1]

The place of power

In embracing the message of the cross, Christians also embrace the way of the cross. The paradox of the message of the cross accompanies those who seek to communicate the liberating story of Jesus. It produces a basic dilemma for those who engage in mission. Because the heart of the Christian message points to the destruction of false powers that are replaced by the freeing power of God, the means by which mission is directed are as important as the message itself. In Christian mission the ends can never justify the means. The wrong means communicate the wrong message. The use of dominating, manipulative power can never result in the establishment of the kingdom of God.

This was hardly a problem in the early life of the church. For centuries, Christians were acutely aware of the possibility of persecution, of suffering and even of death. They were a despised minority. No-one became a convert in order to further their career or social standing. But the dramatic change of status for the church produced by the Edict of Toleration issued by the Emperor Constantine in 313 AD, changed more than just the standing of the church in society. Having been the victim of persecution, the church on occasion used the tools of persecution against those who opposed its message.

It is too frequently the case that Nonconformists, themselves the victims of persecution or at least discrimination in past times, tend to read the history of the church as fatally corrupted by the action of Constantine, as if the pre-Constantinian church lived in a perennial golden age. In fact whole kingdoms had been Christian before the age of Constantine, for example Armenia. But it is nevertheless true that the unique privileges bestowed on the Western church by Constantine introduced new problems of a kind which it had not encountered previously. Thereafter the relationship of the church and its mission to the temptations offered by temporal power and influence have remained a source of tension and debate.

It is an arguable point as to whether the solution offered by the period which we know as Christendom owed its inspiration to an earlier Constantinian model or whether it drew more immediately from the challenge of an Islamic theocracy. But whichever is the case, it is noteworthy that mission hardly existed beyond the confines of Christendom during the period of its ascendancy, apart from the ill-fated activities of the Crusades and an early experiment with mission in China.

Two powerful events in European history were crucial in the gradual end of the medieval world and the emergence of the modern period in Western history. The external event of the discovery of new worlds in the Americas and elsewhere, together with the internal convulsions represented by the Reformation acted as powerful engines of change in the Western world. Both these events had huge implications for the future of missions.

The early response of some missionary activity, notably in the conquest of South America, tended to adopt the model of the crusade. Christendom was to be extended, if necessary by the sword. In this period, both the Reformers and Roman Catholics saw mission as an activity that Church and State engaged in together.[2] Protestants were much slower than Catholics to respond with any major missionary activity. Certainly the earlier settlers in North America sought to share their faith with the inhabitants they encountered, as did the early Dutch settlers in Southern Africa. But little of this activity amounted to a missionary strategy as such. But there was one exception to the general attitude of the Reformers concerning mission. The Anabaptistic tradition, with its strong sense of the separation between Church and State, saw mission in a very different light. For them the whole world was a mission field, both a corrupt Christendom and elsewhere. The church could not be reformed, it had to be restored.

That early tradition was further strengthened by the later Pietist movements on the continent, in particular the Moravians, so influential in the life of John Wesley. Finally, as I have already argued, the vigorous eighteenth- and nineteenth-century revival movements in both North America and Britain provided a powerful motivation for a missionary movement that already existed amongst some Anabaptist and Pietistic groups. It was the emergence of the more powerful movements that sprang directly or indirectly from the impetus of revival that gave rise to what we now call the modern missionary movement. But the emergence of this at the centre of nations which were themselves experiencing dramatic industrial, social and political change and expansion reintroduced the earlier issue of power. The Anabaptist and Pietist traditions had been minority voices. They had engaged in mission despite their status and not because of it. The modern missionary movement drew on their inspiration but it did not take long to make a connection between the expansion of Empire and the growth of mission.

In his excellent treatment of the relationship between missions and colonialism, Brian Stanley offers the present judgement of many in reflecting on the past: 'Delegates to the Fifth Assembly of the World Council of Churches in Nairobi in 1975 were told that the missionaries came to Africa with "the Bible in one hand and the gun in the other".'[3]

We might find that judgement to be something of an overstatement. Certainly some African writers, such as Lamin Sanneh, believe that Western Christians misjudge their role because of an unhealthy degree of guilt concerning the role of missions.[4] But even if we accept this overreaction on the part of Western Christians, the fact remains that the linkage of Western mission, not just to the power of empire but perhaps more importantly to the colonialising power of the culture of the Enlightenment, then we can acknowledge that the issue of the use of power, even if it is not the power of the gun, is a sensitive question in the modern missionary period.

Christopher Smith, in a detailed and perceptive paper on the work of William Carey and his two colleagues at Serampore in India, notes that the issue of caste was a significant obstacle to evangelism. The solution adopted by these pioneer missionaries was to safeguard the financial future of converts by offering them employment. This certainly seemed a charitable act, given the devastation that faced those who lost caste, home and livelihood because of their confession of Christ. But, as Smith points out:

> . . . as their numbers increased Christian villages were created for them off the property. Such an arrangement made it fairly easy for missionaries to monitor new believers' conduct; but it severely hindered the rooting of Christian faith in some Indian soils . . . Who can tell what might have happened if the missionaries had not been in a position to provide employment or other facilities![5]

This more subtle use of power certainly did characterise the general position of Western missions throughout a good deal of the nineteenth century and for at least part of the twentieth century. But as Sanneh points out, foreign missionaries actually made comparatively few converts. Most converts on the mission field have come through the witness of other national Christians, family and friends.[6] The church at the end of the twentieth century is increasingly the church of the poor, the dispossessed and the powerless. The church is becoming stronger in those parts of the world that do not command a great deal of economic or military power. Even more surprisingly, it is in precisely these situations of the relative powerlessness of the Christian community that the church is growing most dramatically.

But the powerlessness of the Christian community is now

no longer confined to the overseas mission field. The church in the West must now be thought of as a community without the power to determine key areas of public life and policy. The influence of the church in the key areas of education, politics and the media is vastly diminished. For example, in Britain, even though religious education in particular and Christianity in general is supposed to have something of a protected status, this simply does not operate in practice. Many head-teachers tacitly refuse to hold a daily act of Christian worship although this is the law of the land, and there is little evidence that the government is going to act to force them to do so. Despite the wishes of a majority of parents, as expressed in numerous public-opinion polls, and despite the passing of legislation that religious education should be in the main, Christian, this position is taken to mean that Christianity should comprise no more than 51 per cent of the RE curriculum. This deliberate flouting of the intention of Parliament is hardly contested.

Governments in Western lands can no longer be looked to to protect the interests of the Christian community, even if they ever did. There is no longer any special pleading for the position of the church; the interests of others are seen as more important. The Sunday-trading legislation in Britain illustrates what would have been an unthinkable shift only twenty years ago.

The media is significantly less kind, and a blatant bias against Christianity often seems to operate. The *Independent*, one of the more respectable British broadsheet newspapers, recently carried the headline 'Carey delivers parting sermon to empty pews'.[7] It was part of that newspaper's reporting of a tour of China by the Archbishop of Canterbury. The picture conjured up by such a headline is hardly encouraging or flattering. Closer examination of the article revealed that in fact the Archbishop had preached to a congregation of more than 300 in a church that seated approximately 450 people. The meeting had been hurriedly arranged and only publicised by word of mouth, which meant that there were some empty seats. That was hardly the impression conveyed by the headline. This single example of a less-than-helpful headline is hardly the worst case of the way in which the media in general treats Christianity in the West, yet is symptomatic of a situation where the media believes it has almost a duty to report Christianity in a negative light. In general terms the treatment of the church emphasises the fact that Christianity is no longer in a situation of privilege in anything but a marginal way in Western lands.

But does this loss of power in the sense of influence in society really matter? Certainly, if we are to think in terms of winning the West it is a consideration which must be weighed. The very language, 'winning the West' can sound militaristic or at least triumphalist in tone. That same language is echoed in some contemporary hymnody. 'Now is the time for us to march upon the land — into our hands he will give the ground we claim.'[8] But a closer examination of that same imagery suggests an acknowledgement that the church in the West is indeed weak. The power that is spoken of is not the power of privilege so much as the power of God, bestowed on the church for the purpose of bringing liberation to all, not the subjugation of some.

This emphasis on the power of God tends to suggest that the loss of power in the sense of privilege might even be something that the church might rejoice over. To the extent that the loss of a power to coerce is replaced by a focus on the power to build communities that flows from genuine repentance and humility, then the relative powerlessness of the church in the West might actually be a cause for hope in the context of mission. The power of a message to transform lives will need to be more important than the power of an institution to control lives. It is for this reason that what happens in the life of the local congregation is so important. The message of the church will need to be seen to reflect

God's redeeming power in its everyday life if the message of the gospel is ever to act as a liberating and creative force in the context of the mission field of the West. What happens at a congregational level will be of tremendous importance for the mission of the church. In this area, there have been some significant changes in recent years.

The recovery of the congregation

The late nineteenth century and early twentieth century probably represent the time of greatest strength for denominational life in the Western world. In England, even the national church was forced to begin to mirror the organisational life of the various Nonconformist denominations. The doctrinal differences between denominations were seen as sufficiently important that when a person moved to another town or city they would usually look for another congregation belonging to the same denomination, or even consider beginning one if one did not already exist. During the nineteenth century the growth of the denomination in which I was brought up followed the growth of the railway system and the mining villages. As the branch lines extended and as new mines were opened, so new congregations followed the move of those who were already committed members of that denomination. The names of the founders of these churches can be traced moving from church to church with the migration of industry.

The strength of denominational life not only stimulated local congregational life, it also led to a view of the importance of the denominational headquarters. The minister of a small congregation often saw a career progression as one which involved moving to a large congregation and eventually to a position of leadership in the denomination as a whole. By the middle of the twentieth century, the strength of the centre almost produced a situation whereby the national expression of denominational life tended to view itself as somehow 'the real church' with the congregations existing in order to support the centre.

That trend is not nearly as pronounced today, especially in Nonconformist denominations. The local congregation has made a comeback with the result that, increasingly, the denomination can only be justified by the degree to which it genuinely serves local congregational life. It is almost the case that denominations are having to redefine themselves as serving networks in order to have any significant meaning.

In part, this shift reflects a broader, world-wide, cultural shift towards decentralisation in many aspects of life. Since the second Vatican Council, even the highly centralised Roman Catholic church has seen a shift in emphasis from a uniformity which looks to the centre towards a diversity of expression which looks increasingly to the local.[9] But an additional factor is also the very success of the church in its mission around the world. The entry of the church into many cultures has been made possible by the way in which it has set its activities in the context of local culture — hence its diversity — and has in turn further encouraged the church to understand itself in terms of a broad unity expressed in local diversity. The congregation has been the focus for mission in those parts of the world where the church is growing rapidly.

The concept of the congregation as the place of mission has also begun to feature strongly in the changing church in the more difficult climate of the Western world. A shift of emphasis in relation to the work of the local church can be seen very clearly in the activity of a number of parachurch agencies. Organisations such as Youth With A Mission, which have often been associated with evangelistic initiatives amongst groups in society which seemed to be unreached by the local church, have shifted their strategic emphasis towards an active policy of church planting. Other groups such as Youth for Christ and Campus Crusade for

Christ (Agape in some countries) have moved towards a policy of a much stronger partnership with local churches. Other specialist agencies, which sometimes tended to see the local church as a means of providing funds to enable the agencies to engage in work in place of the local church, have increasingly looked towards a policy of establishing a stronger partnership with the local church by providing programmes and materials to help the local church to engage in mission directly.

A major cause of this renewal of the congregation is almost certainly the growing strength of the evangelical and Charismatic wing of the church. There have been both pragmatic and theological factors that have helped to produce such an emphasis. In England, evangelicals within the Church of England have for long felt that their path to promotion was effectively blocked by a broadly liberal-catholic establishment. Building a sizeable parish church offered the only real alternative to advancement within the ranks of the church. Evangelicals have had some notable role models in men such as John Stott as an encouragement in taking such a route. A strong theological commitment to evangelism as a priority for the local church is likely to result in local growth. But the commitment to the congregation goes deeper than such obvious factors. The gradual perception that Christendom has now ended, permanently and irrevocably, has had its impact on the way in which Christians view the church. The concept of the church as the gathered and committed people of God, identifiably different from the wider society in which the church is set, has helped to renew the sense of the importance of the congregation. The strengthening of the local church is now both an aim of mission and a means of further extending the mission of the church.

The industrialisation of the West has accompanied the ending of Christendom. The simple fact that the majority of people in Western lands now live in or near cities rather than in a rural setting has forced a major adaptation of congregational models. At first this was not so. While it was always the case that the more important cities contained a few congregations which were larger and more prestigious than the norm, these were always regarded as occasional and acceptable exceptions; the outcome of a gifted preacher — a Spurgeon, a Weatherhead or a Moody. The growth of suburbia meant that the majority of churches would be community churches, designed and adapted to serve the needs of that immediate part of the wider city life. In one sense, just as suburbia was intended to provide city dwellers with a sense of the rural near the city, so suburban churches were almost seen as slightly more sophisticated rural churches. Rural models prevailed in much of suburbia, seen clearly in the successful transfer of occasions such as harvest festival.

But the changing pattern of city life has served to weaken the sense of community that has existed in suburbia. Many city communities now exist merely as dormitory areas. Community as a set of human relationships is now defined in ways other than geography. Increased mobility means that people no longer work, shop, build friendships, are educated and socialise within walking distance, in the way that they once did. This process has weakened the concept of the church as an entirely community church. The parish system in cities has largely broken down, with worshippers crossing such artificial barriers in order to worship in a church that reflects their values, beliefs and worship style in much the same way that they travel to form other social relationships.

This trend has reinforced the concept of the church as a gathered congregation. It has also given rise to some new expressions of the congregation in the twentieth century. Not the least of these expressions is what has been called the 'megachurch' and now, more recently, the metachurch. Although there is no precise definition of either of these terms, a megachurch is usually thought of as one which exceeds 1000 people in worship each week and a meta-church is one which has many thousands of worshippers, perhaps in excess of 10,000. Although these larger churches are often thought of as an American phenomenon, in fact the largest churches in the world are to be found in parts of Asia, Latin America and Africa. The megachurch has now made its appearance both in North America and in Europe. Great Britain has at least seventeen congregations in Protestant churches with an attendance of more than 1000 on a Sunday and Germany has nineteen. Megachurches can be found in almost every European country. There is every reason to believe that the megachurch is both here to stay and that it has a key role to play in mission.

In the context of an increasingly secular society where the power of the church in that society is now almost entirely absent, the megachurch makes at least four important con-tributions to mission. First, it is usually a repository of tremendous creativity and ability. Whether we like it or not, many people who have creative ability are often attracted to the megachurch as worshippers. Their gifts are needed to communicate the Christian message in a secular environment, and the megachurch knows how to use such giftedness. Second, its very size and visibility demands attention. In a situation where the church has been margin-alised, the megachurch refuses to accept such a position. Third, the megachurch is able to marshall the resources that are required, in both financial and people terms, to make an impact amongst unchurched people. The mega-church is able to operate programmes and events that smal-ler churches could not conduct effectively. Fourth, the megachurch can offer the all-important ingredient of anon-ymity for the inquiring secular person who is beginning to express an interest in the Christian faith.[10]

The rise of the megachurch provides one powerful indica-tor of the extent to which local congregational life has made an important and welcome recovery. It mirrors the extent to which the renewal of congregational life is a feature of evangelical and charismatic Christianity. I have been unable to find a single megachurch in Western Europe that does not fit some combination of the description 'evangelical', 'charismatic' or 'Pentecostal'. Indeed, the largest single congregations in cities as diverse as London, Copenhagen, Zurich and Paris are all Pentecostal churches, and that pattern of growth can be repeated in many cities across Europe. As more than one observer has noted, in Europe, the State churches have the buildings but the evangelicals and Pentecostals have the people.

Beyond the congregation

The recovery of the congregation is undoubtedly a powerful factor in the revitalisation of mission in the West. Indeed, it is important to state that the West cannot be won without the vital component of vibrant local congregations. Yet the very identification of mission with the local church raises the danger of seeing the creation of local congregations as the end to which mission is dedicated rather than the means by which mission is accomplished. It is vital to remind ourselves that the goal of mission is the reconciliation of the world to God. The implication of such a goal has usually been taken to mean that mission will have some impact on society and not end merely as a succession of church-growth statistics.

The recovery of the congregation has tended to focus attention on evangelism — by which is meant the conversion of individuals. But the task of mission cannot be restricted to evangelism alone. It has to include some concern for evangelisation — the changing of culture and society in the West — if the West is to be won.[11] The quest for evangelisation is properly the task of the whole church and not just of individual congregations.

In Chapter 9 I commented that, so far, the co-operation which is now evident amongst evangelicals has been mostly restricted to the field of evangelism. In the same chapter we saw that this was not always so. Indeed, rather curiously, the Evangelical Alliance was not formed to help evangelicals with evangelism so much as to strengthen and encourage evangelicals to produce change in society.

But it is precisely at this point that the question of how power is used becomes so critical in the debate about mission. What are we talking about when we talk of evangelisation? Is this really a subtle concern to restore an older Christendom and in so doing to move back to a time when the church seemed to have tremendous power and influence in society?

Leaving aside the fact that, however alluring the past might seem, it can never be recreated, it is vital for the mission of the church in the West that Christians look forward to the growing debate about how our world might be ordered rather than look back fondly to any particular past. But that does not mean that we cannot and should not learn from the past, especially in the matter of how power is approached.

The historian John Wolffe has made a detailed study of religion and national life in Great Britain and Ireland in the nineteenth and twentieth centuries.[12] He offers a convincing analysis of the misuse of power on the part of the church in general and of evangelicals in particular. While recognising that secularisation had produced an alternative cultural expression for many Britons, Wolffe has tried hard to understand how popular religion has functioned during these two centuries. He makes the telling point that the fatal linkage of Christianity with nationalism, imperialism and war severely limited the moral authority with which Christians sought to address the culture. For example, he documents in some detail the shift in attitudes to war amongst Christians at the beginning of the nineteenth-century to those which prevailed by the time of the First World War. At the height of the revivals, evangelicals saw war as 'an unmitigated evil'.[13] From such a standpoint, evangelicals owed a prior loyalty to Christ rather than to the State. By the end of the century there had emerged a degree of identification between the aims of Empire and the cause of Christ in the minds of many evangelicals.

This shift in attitudes reflected what Wolffe describes as a fourfold response to the Christian movement. First, a significant minority could be described as 'enthusiastic receivers'. A second, very small, group fall into the category of outright rejectors. A third and large group he describes as diffuse acceptors. That is to say, they saw Christianity as concerned with advocating a generalised goodness. In these terms, Christianity was seen as a good thing. Jesus was a good man who helped people to become good. Good people could be expected to go to heaven. A fourth and relatively small group are characterised as sectarian adherents. This group consists of those who saw themselves culturally as Catholics or even members of the Church of England and who wore their religious adherence as a kind of cultural badge. Members of the Orange Lodge or British Israelites might be expected to form part of this group. In these terms, the latter two groups often descended into a kind of vapid nationalism which saw Christianity as part of what it meant to be 'civilised' or 'Western' or even more narrowly as 'British'.

One interpretation of Wolffe's argument is that the churches were too often tempted to yield to an interpretation of Christianity that, in effect, embraced a diffuse understanding of the Christian faith to gain a position of national influence and power, which in the end undermined the moral and spiritual authority of Christianity. In this sense, the present emasculation of the power and influence of the church can be welcomed if it means an opportunity to reinterpret what Christianity might have to say to our present culture.

In such a situation, the role of the congregation is vitally important in developing the culture of those who are 'enthusiastic receivers'. But the lessons of the immediate past indicate that there is also a vital role for the whole church in reaching out to those beyond congregational life to hold out a valid vision of what it means to develop a society which is in some important sense 'Christian' in its ideals and aspirations.

Surveying the futures

In assessing the history of world Christianity during the twentieth-century, two major scenarios are suggested for the twenty-first century. The first scenario suggests that the experience of Europe, deepening secularisation and the development of a culture hostile to Christianity, represents the future for the rest of the world. Some observers claim that the secularism of the West has already been exported to many other parts of the world and is even now present in city culture the world over. There is a good deal of evidence to support this view. It is a fact that even in Africa many of those who have been church attenders in rural areas migrate to the cities and never connect with a church. There are many similarities between such situations and the story of Europe in the late eighteenth and early nineteenth centuries.

The second scenario is radically different. It suggests that the rapid progress of Christianity in many parts of the world, particularly through revival movements, but generally through the witness of individual Christians who are members of highly committed local churches, represents the future for the West, especially Europe. Which of these very different possibilities comes nearest to the truth? Is the decline of religious life in Europe the norm for others, the future waiting to happen, or is it merely a temporary aberration, a hiccup of history, that will rejoin the mainstream in the very near future?

My suggestion is that both of these predictions have some validity but in very different ways. Not only is Europe and the West in general exporting a secular culture by means of technological, scientific, commercial, media and educative channels, but also the West itself, at least at the level of government and media, continues to throw off the restraints of a past Christian culture and adopt what appears to be an increasingly secular stance. However, closer examination reveals that while the position of government and media might appear to be more and more secular, particularly because Christianity no longer appears as a privileged player in the dominant culture, what is actually emerging is not a completely secular landscape so much as a number of aspects of secularism, in particular pluralism.

The future of the West is not becoming more secular and less religious. On the contrary, there is every reason for believing that the West is becoming more and more religious but less and less Christian. The development of a pluralistic approach to religious expression is both cause and result of a situation in which Christianity is becoming merely a competitor in a very diverse religious environment. Increasingly, the West is exporting post-modernity as much as modernity. That post-modern paradigm makes room for the expression and validity of religious experience provided that it is not willing to make any absolute claims for itself. Across the world the occult is being reinvented in a post-modern setting. The tarot expert in San Francisco, Singapore, Taipei and Paris uses the convenience of a computer. Modernity interfaces dramatically with the religious traditions of the past in the new post-modern paradigm. Witchcraft in the form of Wicca is increasingly commanding air time in the Western media. Who could have imagined that the Western world, which at the beginning of the twentieth century used the dual message of the Enlightenment and Christianity to ridicule and emasculate witchcraft in Africa and elsewhere, would give serious attention to that same tradition by means of the most advanced technology available at the end of that same century?

If what the West is now exporting is not simply a secular world-view but an increasingly pluralistic post-modernity, is it any nearer the truth to argue that the dramatic growth of Christianity world-wide will soon come to the West, just as it has in Eastern Europe following the collapse of communism? Possibly.

Arguably, Christianity in the past has tended to thrive when placed in a situation of genuine pluralism. The situation of the church in the ancient world during the first three centuries of its life provides ample evidence for such a claim. Equally, the growth of the church during the present century in situations where the dominant religious tradition, such as Islam, is not upheld by the apparatus of the State, demonstrates that under pluralistic conditions, Christianity tends to grow. However, such vibrant growth does not result where Christianity merely appeals to a privileged past. If Christianity is to flourish in the present mission field of the West several conditions will need to be in evidence. In my book *The Faith of the Unbeliever*, I suggest that there are three key questions that the church will need to address if it is to be effective as a missionary church. I listed these as the rediscovery of its message, the re-examination of the role of the Bible and the recovery of the congregation as a vibrant community. These are both practical and theological questions with which the church will need to grapple even as it is engaged in mission. But beyond these questions there are three signs which will indicate to us that the church has begun such a quest.

1. Spiritual power

What is meant by such a term? What is spiritual power? I am not referring to the rather primitive desire to control the elemental forces of the universe — to offer propitiation to the gods. Rather, a religion, or even an experience or an idea, has spiritual power when it offers meaning to the lives of those who embrace it. The forces of the universe do not have to be controlled, but the puzzle of the world in which we live needs to be explained at least at an existential level. Who am I? What is my significance? How can I make sense of the primary relationships in my life? How are pain, struggle, suffering and death approached? The fundamental response of technology is to insist that these questions are not worth asking — they are not real questions. Such a response is simply inadequate. But we have to be honest and admit that the church in the West has been so beguiled by the power of technology, at least to offer relief from suffering and pain, that it has sometimes experienced a temporary amnesia as to the potential power of the Christian message itself. The recovery of spiritual encounter, whether in the form of meditation and the spiritual disciplines or in spiritual ecstasy, has helped clergy and laity alike grapple again with spiritual weapons grown rusty with disuse.

2. Breakthrough congregations

For many years, evangelical Christians have prayed for the coming of revival. I have been one of them. But the problem with such prayers is that they often look backwards to what has been as much as forwards to what might be. Revival, almost by definition, has to do with the recovery of that which has been present in the past. Genuine revival almost always brings something new. A missionary church will tend to create forms of the church which have not been seen before. Certainly there will be some familiar ingredients but the actual forms of worship, of leadership structures and of evangelism will not be so familiar. The recovery of the congregation described earlier in this chapter is tending to produce new forms of the church.

At this stage what really matters is not evidence that large numbers of people are becoming Christians, so much as signs that there really are some situations which might be described as 'breakthrough congregations'. These congregations will be reaching communities of people that have not previously responded to the gospel. They might be alienated sections of the working class, or they might be Muslim communities, or even middle-class professionals whose encounter with Christianity never extended beyond school assemblies. The significance of such breakthrough congregations does not lie in the immediate size of their meetings but in their potential for exponential growth. The dramatic missionary stories of the twentieth century in places such as Mizoram or South Korea looked very uneventful in the first few years of the breakthrough. But in retrospect, what really mattered was not the large numbers of converts that came later so much as the nature of the breakthrough events themselves.

3. The vision of a new society

So far we can be fairly certain that the growth of the evangelical/charismatic community in Western Christianity is sufficiently strong that it has been able to build a strong subculture able to resist the pressures that come from a more hostile environment for Christianity within Western culture. The creation of significant pan-evangelical alliances raises the question as to whether this movement will be able to influence society more generally. The existence of these alliances or coalitions will certainly have the effect of strengthening the evangelical community itself, but the fundamental goal of such strategic groupings is to accomplish much more than this. But can the growing evangelical community have the effect of influencing society more widely? There are some indications which suggest that the combined effect of the growth of the evangelical constituency and a re-evaluation of theological positions more widely in the church is bringing a redefinition of the mainstream in Christianity in the West. Evangelicals have made important overtures to those who would regard themselves as orthodox or credal Christians but who in previous years might have stood closer to a dominant liberal theological centre and who have previously regarded evangelicals as belonging on the fringe of church life.

Even more remarkable, some evangelicals, though by no means all, both in the United States and in parts of Europe, have begun to consider practical alliances with Roman Catholics, whom they regard as taking a much stronger biblical stance on some social and doctrinal issues. This remarkable development could place evangelical Christianity at the forefront of a redefined missionary thrust in the West. However, the success of this enterprise is vitally dependent on the growth of a social agenda amongst evangelicals that would produce a vision for a new society. There has been growing evidence for some years that such a vision is becoming an increasingly important part of an evangelical agenda. A working relationship with Roman Catholics might well help to strengthen such a vision.

Historians are always anxious to remind futurologists that human experience has been marked by the totally unexpected. The recent history of the West has been no exception to this tendency in the tide of human affairs. The immediate future is likely to be just as puzzling as the immediate past. The signposts for the future of mission in the West will continue to point confusingly in more than one direction before we can be sure of a broader tendency. Almost certainly there will come a deepening secularisation in the West with even greater difficulties for the Christian community. Equally there will be a growing openness to spiritual issues.

Some parts of the church in the West will continue to suffer decline and even some desperation as they face the future. But other, seemingly insignificant events, possibly hidden from sight to the casual observer, will herald a potentially different outcome for the mission of the church in the West. So far the signs that point to the winning of the West are small, but the very fact that they are there at all is vitally important. The dawning of the day will reveal much that transpired in the labours of the night.

Notes

1. Walter Wink, *Engaging the Powers*, p. 140.
2. David Bosch, *Transforming Mission*, pp. 227, 246.
3. Brian Stanley, *The Bible and the Flag*, p. 11.
4. Lamin Sanneh, *Go*, Jan–March 1991, 'Christian Missions and the Western Guilt Complex', p. 6.
5. Christopher Smith, 'Mythology and Missiology: A Methodological approach to the Pre Victorian Mission of the Serampore Trio', *IRM* Vol. LXXXIII, pp. 462ff.
6. *Ibid.*
7. 'Carey Delivers Parting Sermon to Empty Pews', *Independent*, 20 September 1994, p. 9.
8. Graham Kendrick, *Rejoice, rejoice* © Thankyou Music, 1983. Words quoted from *Mission Praise* 572.
9. Shorter Aylward, *Evangelisation and Culture*, pp. 112ff.
10. Willow Creek Community Church in Chicago represents the best-known example of this approach amongst megachurches.
11. William Abrahams argues that there really is no difference between evangelism and evangelisation.
12. John Wolffe, *God and Greater Britain*.
13. *Ibid.*, p. 41.

BIBLIOGRAPHY

Allen, Roland. *The Spontaneous Expansion of the Church and the Causes Which Hinder it.* World Dominion Press: 1960.

Arnal, Oscar L. *Priests in Working-Class Blue: The History of the Worker-Priests 1943–1954.* Paulist Press: 1986.

Barker, Eileen. *New Religious Movements: A Practical Introduction.* HMSO: 1989.

Barrett, David B. *The World Christian Encyclopedia.* OUP: 1982.

Bebbington, D. W. *Evangelicalism in Modern Britain: A History from the 1730s to the 1980s.* Unwin Hyman: 1989.

Bilheimer, Robert S. *Breakthrough: The Emergence of the Ecumenical Tradition.* Eerdmans: 1989.

Boddy, Alexander, *To Kai the Holy.* Kegan Paul Trench & Co: 1885.

Bonk, Jonathan J. *Mission and Money: Affluence as a Western Missionary Problem.* Orbis: 1991.

Bosch, David. *Transforming Mission: Paradigm Shifts in Theology of Mission.* Orbis: 1991.

Burnett, David. *Dawning of the Pagan Moon.* Monarch: 1991.

Carpenter, Joel Al and Shenk, Wilbert R. (eds.). *Earthen Vessels: American Evangelicals and Foreign Missions, 1880–1980.* Eerdmans: 1990.

Clarke, John. *Evangelism that really works.* SPCK: 1995.

Coote, Robert T. and Phillips, James M. (eds.). *Towards the 21st Century in Christian Mission.* Eerdmans: 1993.

Cronin, A. J. *The Keys of the Kingdom.* Victor Gollancz: 1941/New English Library: 1972.

Dempster, Murray A., Klaus, Byron D., and Petersen, Douglas

(eds.). *Called and Empowered: Global Mission in Pentecostal Perspective.* Hendrikson Publishers: 1991.

Douglas, J. D. (ed.). 'Proclaim Christ Until He Comes: Calling the Whole Church to Take the Whole Gospel to the Whole World.' *Lausanne II in Manila, International Congress on World Evangelization, 1989.* World Wide Publications: 1990.

Drane, John. *Evangelism for a New Age.* Marshall Pickering: 1994.

Ellul, Jacques. *The New Demons.* The Seabury Press: 1975.

Fey, Harold (ed.). *A History of the Ecumenical Movement, Vol. 2, 1948–1968.* Second edition. World Council of Churches/SPCK: 1986.

Foster, Charles I, *An Errand of Mercy.* The Evangelical United Front, 1790–1837, Chapel Hill: 1960.

Harvey, David. *The Condition of Postmodernity.* Blackwell: 1989.

Hastings, Adrian. *The World Mission of the Church.* Darton, Longman and Todd: 1964.

Hastings, Adrian. *African Catholicism: Essays in Discovery.* SCM: 1989.

Hastings, Adrian. *A History of English Christianity 1920–1990.* Third edition. SCM: 1990.

Hedlund, Roger E. *Evangelization and Church Growth: Issues from the Asian Context.* CGRC, McGavran Institute, India: 1992.

Hollenweger, Walter. *The Pentecostals.* SCM: 1972.

Hollenweger, Walter. *Pentecost Between Black and White.* Christian Journals Ltd: 1974.

Hollenweger, Walter. *Evangelism Today.* Christian Journals Ltd: 1976.

't Hooft, Visser. *Memoirs.* WCC Publications: 1973.

Koop, Allen V. *American Evangelical Missionaries in France 1945–1975.* University Press of America: 1986.

Kraft, Charles. *Christianity in Culture:* A Study in Dynamic Biblical Theologyzing in Cross-Cultural Perspective. Orbis: 1994.

Kung, Hans. *Christianity, the Religious Situation of Our Time.* SCM: 1995.

McGrath, Alister. *Bridge Building: Effective Christian Apologetics.* IVP: 1992.

McGrath, Alister. *Evangelicalism and the Future of Christianity.* Hodder and Stoughton: 1993.

Montgomery, Jim. *DAWN 2000: 7 Million Churches to go.* William Carey Library, Pasedena: 1989.

Myers, Bryant L. *The Changing Shape of World Mission.* MARC: 1993.

Neill, Stephen. *A History of Christian Missions.* Penguin: 1964.

Newbigin, Lesslie. *The Household of God.* SCM: 1953.

Newbigin, Lesslie. *The Gospel in a Pluralist Society.* SPCK: 1989.

Noll, Mark A. *A History of Christianity in the United States and Canada.* SPCK: 1992.

Pannenberg, W. *Christianity in a Secularised World.* SCM: 1988.

Pointer, Roy. *How do Churches Grow?: A Guide to the Growth of Your Church.* Marshall, Morgan & Scott: 1984.

Robinson, Martin. *Two Winds Blowing.* M.Litt thesis for Birmingham University: 1976.

Robinson, Martin. *A World Apart.* Monarch: 1992.

Robinson, Martin and Christine, Stuart. *Planning Tomorrow's Churches Today.* Monarch: 1992.

Robinson, Martin and Yarnell, Dan. *Celebrating the Small Church.* Monarch: 1993.

Robinson, Martin. *The Faith of the Unbeliever.* Monarch: 1994.

Robinson, Martin. *To the Ends of the Earth* – the Pilgrimage of an Ecumenical Pentecostal, Doctoral thesis for Birmingham University: 1987.

Rouse, Ruth and Neill, Stephen (eds.). *A History of the Ecumenical Movement, Vol. 1, 1517–1948.* Third edition. World Council of Churches: 1986.

Sacks, Jonathan. *The Persistence of Faith: Religion, Morality and Society in a Secular Age.* Weidenfeld Paperbacks: 1991.

Sanneh, Lamin in *Toward the 21st Century* in *Christian Mission* (eds. J. M. Philips and R. T. Coate), Eerdmans 1993.

Shorter, Aylward. *Evangelisation and Culture.* Geoffrey Chapman: 1994.

Stanley, Brian. *The Bible and the Flag: Protestant Missions and British Imperialism in the Nineteenth and Twentieth Centuries.* Apollos: 1990.

Sundkler, Bengt. *Bantu Prophets in South Africa.* Second edition. OUP: 1961.

Sundkler, Bengt. *Zulu Zion and Some Swazi Zionists.* OUP: 1976.

Tidball, Derek. *Who are the Evangelicals?: Tracing the Roots of Today's Movements.* Marshall Pickering: 1994.

Wagner, William L. *North American Protestant Missionaries in Western Europe: A Critical Appraisal.* VKW, Stuttgart: 1993.

Walls, Andrew. Friends of St Colm's Public Lecture, 21 May 1989. St Colm's Education Centre and College: 1989.

Ward, W. R. *Faith and Faction.* Epworth: 1993.

Warren, Max. *Social History and Christian Mission.* SCM: 1967.

Warren, Robert. *Building Missionary Congregations.* Church House Publishers: 1995.

Wessels, Anton. *Europe: Was it Ever Really Christian?* SCM: 1994.

Wilson, Everett. *Called and Empowered:* Global Mission in Pentecostal Perspective, (eds. M. A. Dempster, B. D. Klaus and D. Petersen). Hendrickson: 1991.

Wink, Walter. *Engaging the Powers: Discernment and Resistance in a World of Domination.* Fortress Press: 1992.

Wolffe, John. *God and Greater Britain: Religion and National Life in Britain and Ireland 1843–1945.* Routledge: 1994.

Wuthnow, Robert. *Christianity in the 21st Century: Reflections on the Challenges Ahead.* OUP: 1993.

Yates Timothy. *A History of Christian Missions in the Twentieth Century.* Cambridge University Press: 1994.

INDEX

Brethren 47; Plymouth 116
Britain, British 17, 22, 37–39, 41, 43,
49, 51, 53, 67, 76–78, 82–83, 103–
105, 109, 113–114, 118, 120–125,
127, 144, 151, 165f., 187, 192, 194,
206–207, 225, 227, 233, 235–236
British and Foreign Bible Society 43, 46
British General Election of 1945 67
Bruce, F. F. 121
Bryan, William Jennings 117
Buddhism 73–74, 88, 157f.
Burma 103

Caesar, cult of 19–20
Calvinists 14
Cambridge 40
Campus Crusade for Christ 172, 187,
231
Canada 103
Canberra 99
Cape Town 49–50
Carey, George 227
Carey, William 44, 49–50, 226
Carter, President Jimmy 124
Celtic church 22–23
Challenge 2000 192
charismatic movement 101, 124, 128,
145, 147–148, 150, 152, 179,
194–197, 231, 234, 241
Chartist movement 40
Chaucer, Geoffrey 30
Chile 139
China, Chinese 88, 91, 134, 142, 224,
227
Christendom 23–27, 30, 32, 34, 54, 72,
106–107, 109, 156–157, 211, 224,
231, 235
Christianity *passim*; catholic stream
148–149
Church of England 32, 39–41, 46, 50–
51, 62, 100, 113, 122–123, 126, 152,
206, 231, 236; Anglo-Catholicism 40,
50, 54, 61, 96; Broad Church 40
Church of God in Christ 138
Church Fathers 20, 26, 29
Church Missionary Society 77
church, churches *passim*; co-operation
among 14, 48, 50–55, 58, 102, 191–
197, 235; decline of 63–65, 104;
divisions in 14, 32–33, 45, 48, 54, 65;

early 19–20, 26, 29, 42, 223, 239;
future of 237–243; growth of 12, 14,
18, 20, 28, 39, 41–42, 44, 80–81, 83,
86–89, 91, 103–104, 119–12, 122,
125, 134f., 136, 180, 205–206, 226,
230–231, 234, 239, 241; history of
11, 14, 17, 28, 31, 35, 53, 237;
interculturalism of 28–29, 33, 35;
leadership in 13, 32, 44, 46–47, 49, 59,
62, 78–79, 82, 84, 141, 182, 205–206,
241; local 12–13, 19, 229–234;
planting of 41, 171, 197, 230; union
schemes 103–104; unity of 33, 46–47,
52, 54–55, 100, 104, 112
Churchill, Winston 67
cities 19, 22, 37–39, 232, 237
'Clapham Sect' 40, 105, 193
clergy 34–35
colonialism 11–12, 25, 42–43, 73–74,
76–80, 82, 85, 91, 110, 225
Columba, St 17
'comity' agreements 48
communion 10, 31, 35
communism 66–70, 108, 110, 190, 239
Confucianism 88
Congregationalism 39, 46, 127
Conservative Party 32, 67
Constantine, Emperor 44, 223–224
Constantinople 23–24
consumerism 70
contemporary culture 126–127, 203–
205, 234, 237, 241
Co-operative movement 40
conversion 22–23, 25, 30, 39, 44, 136,
140
Copenhagen 91
cosmology 26
Counter Reformation 26, 41
creation 110
Cronin, A. J. 60
cross 223
crusades 25, 224
cultural pluralism 19–20

Darby, John Nelson 116
Darrow, Clarence 117
Darwin(ism) 65, 70, 96, 114
DAWN 131–132
Decade of Evangelism 126, 183, 186,
206